# The PRIESTHOOD POWER of WOMEN

# *The* PRIESTHOOD POWER *of* WOMEN

In the Temple, Church, and Family

BARBARA MORGAN GARDNER

DESERET BOOK

© 2019 Barbara Morgan Gardner

All rights reserved. No part of this book may be reproduced in any form or by any means without permission in writing from the publisher, Deseret Book Company, at permissions@deseretbook.com or PO Box 30178, Salt Lake City, Utah 84130. The views expressed herein are the responsibility of the author and do not necessarily represent the position of Deseret Book Company.

This material is neither made, provided, approved, nor endorsed by Intellectual Reserve, Inc., or The Church of Jesus Christ of Latter-day Saints. Any content or opinions expressed, implied, or included in or with the material are solely those of the owner and not those of Intellectual Reserve, Inc., or The Church of Jesus Christ of Latter-day Saints.

DESERET BOOK is a registered trademark of Deseret Book Company.

Visit us at deseretbook.com

Library of Congress Cataloging-in-Publication Data

Names: Morgan, Barbara E., author.
Title: The priesthood power of women : in the temple, church, and family / Barbara Morgan Gardner.
Description: Salt Lake City, Utah : Deseret Book, 2019. | Includes bibliographical references and index.
Identifiers: LCCN 2019019838 | ISBN 9781629725604 (hardbound : alk. paper)
Subjects: LCSH: Women—Religious aspects—The Church of Jesus Christ of Latter-day Saints. | Priesthood—The Church of Jesus Christ of Latter-day Saints. | Priesthood—Mormon Church. | Women and religion.
Classification: LCC BX8643.W66 M667 2019 | DDC 289.3/32082—dc23
LC record available at https://lccn.loc.gov/2019019838

Printed in the United States of America
Publishers Printing, Salt Lake City, UT

10  9  8  7  6  5  4  3

*To my parents,
Sharon Elaine LeBaron Morgan
and Alvin Wright Morgan Jr.,
for their faithfulness in seeking and
acting upon divine truth*

# CONTENTS

| | | |
|---|---|---:|
| | Introduction: "For Such a Time as This" . . . . . . . . . . | ix |
| Chapter 1 | Doctrine, History, and Structure of the Priesthood . . . . | 1 |
| Chapter 2 | Priesthood Keys, Authority, and Power in the Church . . | 25 |
| Chapter 3 | "What Other Authority Can It Be?" Connecting Women with Priesthood at Church . . . . . | 45 |
| Chapter 4 | The Temple and the Patriarchal Order of the Priesthood . . . . . . . . . . . . . . . . . . . . . . . | 65 |
| Chapter 5 | "Endowed with Priesthood Power" Connecting Women with Priesthood in the Temple and Home . . . . . . . . . . . . . . . . . . . | 88 |
| Chapter 6 | That We Might Be One . . . . . . . . . . . . . . . . . . . | 112 |
| Chapter 7 | Filling the Measure of Our Creation . . . . . . . . . . . | 129 |
| | Acknowledgments . . . . . . . . . . . . . . . . . . . . . | 139 |
| | Notes . . . . . . . . . . . . . . . . . . . . . . . . . . . . . | 141 |
| | Index . . . . . . . . . . . . . . . . . . . . . . . . . . . . . | 153 |

Introduction

# "FOR SUCH A TIME AS THIS"

One of the landmark policy changes President Thomas S. Monson made as President of the Church was the adjustment in missionary age for young adult women and men.[1] What that decision alone has done for the women of the Church is outstanding. Because more young women are studying and teaching the words of the living prophets and standard works, there are more young women trying to apply the teachings found therein in their own lives. The more spiritually mature are listening to the pleadings of Church leaders to study and know the doctrine of the gospel better and to live their lives based on this revealed truth. More young women than ever are attending the temple to perform baptisms, and many are receiving their endowments while still teenagers.

I have taught religion for more than two decades now, and since the change in missionary age, I have heard more questions in class and in my office regarding women, the priesthood, the temple, and family responsibilities than ever before. Young women are asking incredibly insightful and pertinent questions and trying to better understand how the teachings of the temple apply to their lives and to their roles as women in the Church and in their families.

In fact, nearly 75 percent of all of my female students at Brigham Young University have received their temple endowments. These young women are wise, curious, intelligent, doctrinally grounded, and faithful. Their questions are invigorating, exciting, and extremely important. It is not just the returned missionaries that are asking these questions. I was surprised, when I recently served as a stake Young Women president, at how sincerely curious and faithful the young women were. This rising generation has been asked by the prophet to "enlist in the youth battalion of the Lord to help gather Israel."[2] Like President Russell M. Nelson, I too believe that these youth are the best the Lord has ever sent to this earth. They are strong, resilient, obedient, faithful, determined, spiritual, and pure. They are not perfect, but they have what it takes to help in this great gathering. For leaders, teachers, and parents, it is no longer acceptable to simply sidestep some of their difficult questions and bear our testimony.

And it's not just the youth and young adults asking these questions. There has been a surge of women and men searching for answers, and the leaders of the Church are encouraging them along this noble path.

## QUESTIONS REGARDING WOMEN AND THE PRIESTHOOD

Some of the questions I've been hearing include: What is the priesthood? Do women have the priesthood? What is the significance of temple clothing for women? What is my role as a woman in the Church? Why are men the only ones ordained to priesthood offices? What are priesthood keys? How does one obtain priesthood authority? What is the difference between how the priesthood functions in the family and in the Church? What does it mean to preside, and how is presiding determined? If men and women are supposed to be equal partners, why does one preside? What does it mean to nurture? What is priesthood power? How does priesthood apply to women? When women are endowed with priesthood power in the temple, is that the same power received by men? What is the role of the Relief Society in the Church? What is my role as a Relief Society president in calling counselors or working with the elders quorum president? What is the role of women in the salvation of souls? How do we distinguish between the priesthood received by women in the endowment and the priesthood received by men when they are ordained to a priesthood office? What is the role of men and women in the home in regard to covenants made in the temple? Why does any of this matter?

Through the years I have asked and tried to answer these and similar questions in conversations with students and a number of members of the Church. We need to understand these things better. Imagine, for instance, the power that comes to a single sister, or the wife of an inactive or nonmember husband, who realizes that because of the covenants she made in the temple, she has priesthood power in her home. President M. Russell Ballard taught, "When men and women go to the temple, they are both endowed with the same power, which by definition is priesthood power.... Access to the power and the blessings of the priesthood is available to all of God's children."[3] That woman may be blessed by a priesthood holder who comes into her home and performs an ordinance of the priesthood, but she is not without the priesthood.

Imagine the strength of a Primary teacher when she realizes she can make promises to the children in her class because of the priesthood authority that she was

> "When men and women go to the temple, they are both endowed with the same power, which by definition is priesthood power."
> —M. Russell Ballard

given when she was set apart for her calling. Imagine the difference it makes for a mother to know that, as a nurturer, she has the primary responsibility of teaching the gospel in her home. Imagine the strength of a husband and wife, sealed together in the temple, when the two of them realize that together they have entered into the patriarchal order of the priesthood (the new and everlasting covenant of marriage), that each of them is a contributing partner in the creation of an eternal family, as co-equals, without one being the boss over the other.[4]

All members of the Church, especially the women, are the very ones who need to be prepared to teach truths regarding the priesthood. If we don't teach them, who will? Who will answer the questions of the young women when they go through the temple for the first time? Who will accurately prepare the Primary girls for their first calling—which they may receive even while still in Primary—and explain to them that they will have priesthood authority?[5] Who will teach the Primary girls in their temple preparation class about the power of the temple? Who will mentor our daughters and help them through difficult times, especially against the culture of modern society (which we have been told so many times will only get worse), if it is not the mothers, aunts, sisters, and women leaders? Who will help unify the sisters of the world with truth if the faithful and strong sisters do not know and understand true doctrine? How will we as women use the priesthood power we have been endowed with in our homes, communities, and world if we don't know what it is, let alone how to call upon it?

No matter how much we think we know about the gospel, and especially the priesthood, there is obviously much more we need to learn. We study the priesthood because we love it, we want to draw upon its authority and power, and we want to help others be empowered as well. We have testimonies of the living prophets and desire to follow their admonition to better understand and use the power of the priesthood to bless others.

Although this book is focused primarily on helping women better understand the priesthood, I have had many a bishop, seminary or institute teacher, brother, husband, father, or stake president emphasize that this topic needs to be understood by men as well. Anyone who has any leadership or other connection with women (which is likely everyone) will benefit from a deepened understanding of priesthood power. In fact, it has become clear that both men and women need to understand their priesthood privileges in order to accomplish what God would have them do during this, the eleventh hour. I have noticed that President Russell M. Nelson has emphasized our need for a paradigm shift in our thinking about the relationship between the family and the Church as part of our preparation for the Second Coming.[6] In other words, the Church has been instituted to support individuals and families, and not the other way around. As part of that paradigm shift, women must understand and use their priesthood privileges in order for the Lord to accomplish His work on the earth.

Perhaps no one has written more extensively about women in the Church than Sheri Dew, former counselor in the General Relief Society Presidency. In her book *Women and the Priesthood: What One Mormon Woman Believes,* she provides a disclaimer of sorts,[7] which summarizes my sentiments on writing about this topic as well. Like Sister Dew, I recognize that this book will likely not please everyone, and some may even find themselves offended by my writings. I have never felt seriously marginalized by members of the Church or Church leaders, but I also acknowledge that there are those who have, and their feelings are important to me. I recognize that although it is our choice to be offended, it is also our choice to do all we can not to cause offense. Elder Jeffrey R. Holland teaches that "offense is more likely to come in *how* we present the doctrine rather than in the doctrine itself."[8] I hope to be sensitive to both, while still teaching true doctrine. I would also add that I find it extremely important not to come across as a know-it-all or suggest in any way that I consider myself a spokeswoman on this topic for the Church. Rather, I have had many relevant experiences, and I feel a sense of duty to participate positively in the conversation.

I also acknowledge that "I am still learning."[9] It has become clearer and clearer to me that the more I learn about the priesthood, the more I realize I do not know. As I have worked to better understand women and the priesthood, "the eyes of my understanding" (Doctrine and Covenants 138:11) have been opened on many occasions. Some things that used to seem so basic have become complex, and some things I have never understood have become clear. Frankly, as is the case with many authors of many books, it is difficult to be done with the writing of this book, as I know that I will learn more on the topic tomorrow.

In the April 2018 general conference, President Nelson, in his first talk as President of the Church, declared, "Oh, there is so much more that your Father in Heaven wants you to know." To emphasize this point, he quoted Elder Neal A. Maxwell, "To those who have eyes to see and ears to hear, it is clear that the Father and the Son are giving away the secrets of the universe!"[10] I believe, as the scriptures teach, that where "much is

INTRODUCTION

given much is required" (Doctrine and Covenants 82:3), and a topic of such import as the priesthood requires great effort, faith, and patience on our part. President Nelson taught, "Nothing opens the heavens quite like the combination of increased purity, exact obedience, earnest seeking, daily feasting on the words of Christ in the Book of Mormon, and regular time committed to temple and family history work."[11] Since the doctrine of the priesthood is so pronounced in the Doctrine and Covenants, I suggest adding sections 2, 13, 20, 76, 84, 86, 95, 107, 110, 112, 121, 124, 131, and 132 to President Nelson's list when studying this subject, as well as any other prophetic teachings the Spirit would guide you to study.

Elder Bruce R. McConkie instructed: "This doctrine of the priesthood—unknown in the world and but little known even in the Church—cannot be learned out of the scriptures alone. It is not set forth in the sermons and teachings of the prophets and Apostles, except in small measure. The doctrine of the priesthood is known only by personal revelation. It comes, line upon line and precept upon precept, by the power of the Holy Ghost to those who love and serve God with all their heart, might, mind, and strength."[12]

> As members of the Church, especially women, better understand the doctrine of the priesthood, our attitudes and behavior will change.

The importance of covenant women understanding the doctrines of the gospel of Jesus Christ cannot be overestimated. President Boyd K. Packer taught, "True doctrine, understood, changes attitudes and behavior."[13] Note in this statement that it is not only true doctrine existing, or true doctrine known, but true doctrine *understood* that changes attitudes and behavior. Understanding true doctrine comes from a combination of hard work and effort with the Spirit testifying of these truths. As members of the Church, especially women, better understand the doctrine of the priesthood, our attitudes and behavior will change. We will be able to "to step forward! Take [our] rightful and needful place in [our] home, in [our] community, and in the kingdom of God—more than [we] ever have before,"[14] as President Nelson pled for us to do. We will be able to understand and use the priesthood privileges available to us. We will know how to call upon the powers of the priesthood in our own lives, in our families, in our communities, and in the world. We will see God's hand in our lives and have the determination and ability to become like Him and help Him in this great work to gather Israel.

In this book, therefore, we will take a closer look at the priesthood and how it applies to women at Church, in the temple, in the family, and in the larger community by exploring the teachings of current prophets and Apostles and the standard works. We will also take a closer look at what the Brethren are asking the women to do and become, the changes that have been made recently that specifically involve women, and the enhanced role of women in various capacities. Unity between women and men, between adults and youth, and between members of The Church of Jesus Christ of Latter-day Saints and those of other faiths will be critical in the future.

## CONCLUSION

President Heber C. Kimball expressed that "the greatest torment [the Prophet Joseph] had and the greatest mental suffering was because this people would not live up to their privileges. . . . He said sometimes that he felt . . . as though he were pent up in an acorn shell, and all because the people . . . *would not prepare themselves to receive the rich treasures of wisdom and knowledge that he had to impart.* He could have revealed a great many things to us if we had been ready; but he said there were many things that we could not receive because we lacked that diligence . . . necessary to entitle us to those choice things of the kingdom."[15]

Perhaps this struggle of the Prophet Joseph Smith has been passed on from each prophet to the next as they strive to receive the revelation, wisdom, knowledge, and treasures the Lord desires to impart. Most recently, President Russell M. Nelson has admonished, "I urge you to stretch beyond your current spiritual ability to receive personal revelation, for the Lord has promised that 'if thou shalt [seek], thou shalt receive revelation upon revelation, knowledge upon knowledge, that thou mayest know

## INTRODUCTION

the mysteries and peaceable things—that which bringeth joy, that which bringeth life eternal' (Doctrine and Covenants 42:61)."[16]

With that admonition in mind, I invite you to join with me in your personal study, taking careful note of important truths imparted by the Spirit with the intention of acting on and teaching these truths for the salvation of our Heavenly Parents' children.

# Chapter 1

# DOCTRINE, HISTORY, AND STRUCTURE OF THE PRIESTHOOD

Some may remember a story of President Spencer W. Kimball helping a stranded pregnant woman in the airport who was pushing along her young toddler.[1] President Kimball comforted the woman, whom he had never met and knew nothing about, gave the little girl a piece of gum, and got the young, pregnant, exhausted mother and her wet and hungry two-year-old daughter on the next flight out of the Chicago O'Hare airport.

That young pregnant woman was my mother. I have sat in Church meetings when this story was shared, and when members have asked more regarding the backstory. Perhaps a little of the rest of the story could be of benefit in the context of the priesthood and men and women working together for the salvation of souls.

My parents met at Brigham Young University. My mother had been an active member of the Church all her life, although by the time she reached adulthood, her mother had become inactive. My dad was raised in an inactive home. His mother died by suicide when he was a young teenager. Due to the circumstances of his youth, he determined at a young age that he would raise his family differently from how he was raised. My dad basically raised himself as an active member, thanks in great part to the support of wonderful friends and Church leaders. He served a mission for the Lord in the Eastern States, and, to make a long story short, after he returned from his mission, my parents eloped to the Salt Lake Temple, where they were sealed. None of their parents attended.

After their marriage, my parents continued their education at BYU. My mom graduated in elementary education and used her degree to teach school while helping my dad get through school. (She would continue to use her degree throughout the rest of her life, especially in the raising of her children.) While still in school, my mom gave birth to their oldest daughter. Four miscarriages followed, and the doctors put my mom on bed rest, as she had become quite weak with these pregnancies. The doctors tried to convince my parents to not have more children, and even to abort their current unborn baby, but they both felt strongly that they wanted and were inspired to have more children.

Now, with my mom pregnant for the sixth time but extremely weak, my parents decided that it would be best for my dad to drop out of school and my mom to leave work for a while so they could move to Michigan, where my mother could receive help from her family. Not having enough money for all of them to fly, and aware of the danger a long drive would impose on my mom and the baby, my parents sold everything they had: musical instruments, car, clothes, and so on, to get my mom on that airplane with my sister. In fact, my dad had thirty-five cents extra in his pocket that he gave to my mom in case she needed it. Knowing that money would be tight for him, and his drive longer than her flight, she snuck the money back into his coat pocket, just in case. The plan was for my dad, in his junker car, to drop my mom and sister off at the airport and then drive all day and night and meet them in Michigan.

All went as planned until the pilot announced that, due to weather, the plane would have to make an emergency landing in Chicago. Having been instructed by the doctor that she couldn't hold anything heavier than a loaf of bread, and having no money, no extra change of clothes for her or her daughter, no extra food, and no extra diapers, my mom got off the airplane with my sister. Hours went by, and there was no indication of when they would be leaving. My mom was exhausted and concerned. Finding no available seat, she eventually slumped down against a wall with my sister cradled in her lap. In this position, she prayed and pled for help, hoping not to lose this baby and wanting to relieve the burdens of her young daughter.

Within moments, a kind, elderly man came and knelt by them on the floor, assessed the situation, and began offering help. He immediately picked up my soaking wet and sobbing toddler sister and wrapped her in his arms. Carrying my sister, the gentleman went to the desk and, with some type of persuasion, got my mom and sister on the next flight to Michigan. Although my mom did not recognize the man, she later reflected that she should have been more embarrassed for their circumstances, as my sister soaked his suit with her dripping wet diaper and she herself was in a horrible state. But, in the moment, she was overwhelmed with gratitude for the kindness of this elderly gentleman.

Months later, after giving birth to a healthy boy, my parents were at a fireside being broadcast from Salt Lake City. When President Spencer W. Kimball began speaking, my mom immediately recognized him as the man in the airport. She immediately wrote him a letter, thanking him for his service. He responded that he would never forget that day in the airport and thanked *her* for her service as a wife and mother.

My mom was cautious in speaking of this story, never wanting to bring undue attention to herself, always stating that it was President Kimball's story. In many ways it is. But for me, it's also a story of how the Lord uses His priesthood to bless His righteous disciples: President Kimball as a priesthood key holder, and my mom and dad, both endowed with priesthood power and authority for their own family.

President Kimball, as an Apostle of the Lord Jesus Christ, held all the keys of the kingdom of God on the earth in this dispensation. Because of this priesthood authority, he literally could act in the name of God in all things. Because of his righteousness, he was blessed with incredible priesthood power. My mother has mentioned on a number of occasions that, during the time President Kimball was helping her, she literally felt as if he were blessing her—healing her, in a sense. In fact, after this experience with President Kimball, my parents were blessed to have ten more naturally born children, adopted another, and also raised my dad's nephew, whom I know only as my brother. Their ability to rear thirteen children was clearly a miracle and defied all the odds previously pronounced by the doctors.

President M. Russell Ballard taught, "Not only is the priesthood the power by which the heavens and the earth were created, but it is also the power the Savior used in His mortal ministry to perform miracles, to bless and heal the sick, to bring the dead to life, and, as our Father's Only Begotten Son, to endure the unbearable pain of Gethsemane and Calvary—thus fulfilling the laws of justice with mercy and providing an infinite Atonement and overcoming physical death through the Resurrection."[2]

As for my parents, they too were using the power and authority of the priesthood with which they were endowed, having each made and kept sacred covenants in the temple. They had knelt across the altar as a couple and entered into the patriarchal/familial order of the priesthood, or the new and everlasting covenant of marriage, and were both given priesthood power and authority of God for their family. President Ezra Taft Benson explained that "the order of priesthood spoken of in the scriptures is sometimes referred to as the patriarchal order because it came down from father to son. But this order is otherwise described in modern revelation as an order of family government where a man and woman enter into a covenant with God—just as did Adam and Eve—to be sealed for eternity, to have posterity, and to do the will and work of God throughout their mortality."[3]

Both my mom and dad were thus able to receive revelation, knowledge, authority, and power available only to those who make and keep these sacred covenants in the temple. Although traveling alone on the plane, my mother was not without the priesthood power and authority of God, as she was blessed with it in God's holy temple.

Here were three people: President Kimball, my mother, and my father, all using their priesthood power and authority for the salvation of God's children on the earth. These three individuals were determined to keep their covenants, and, in their own unique ways, be about His errand for the salvation of the souls of others. I believe that because of the covenants each of these three members made, and their willingness to serve the Lord and obey Him at all costs, He blessed each of them with priesthood power and authority. It's as if my parents, President Kimball, and the Lord were all on the same team, to "bring to pass the immortality and eternal life of man" (Moses 1:39).

For some, the story of President Kimball helping my mother in the airport is a story of service and charity. For me, it is a story of individuals carefully and wisely using God's priesthood, a true show of charity using God's power. Understanding how each of these three individuals used their priesthood power and authority is absolutely critical for us, women and men alike, in order to fulfill our unique missions on the earth. During his first general conference as the prophet of the Church, President Russell M. Nelson shared the concern that "too many of our brothers and sisters do not fully understand the concept of priesthood power and authority," and that they "do not grasp the privileges that could be theirs."[4] As we come to better understand and apply the teachings regarding the priesthood, we will be able to grasp those privileges.

Elder Dale G. Renlund and Sister Ruth Lybbert Renlund wrote: "Many members of the Church who accept, love, and appreciate the priesthood may find themselves 'fuzzy' on the doctrine and principles. Perhaps that is because the term *priesthood* is used in at least two ways. First, *priesthood* is the term used to describe the total power and authority of God. Second, *priesthood* is also the term used to describe the power and authority that God gives to ordained priesthood holders on earth to act in all things necessary for the salvation of God's children." Continuing, they explain, "Thus, the same word, *priesthood,* refers both to God's total power and authority and to that portion of His power and authority that He delegates to man on earth."[5]

It is the second definition of priesthood that is most commonly taught, but in the process, the larger, more expansive term for *priesthood* is often forgotten or misunderstood. Elder and Sister Renlund compare the way we use the term *priesthood* with the way we use the term *earth*.[6] *Earth* can either be the entire globe upon which all of us live, or it can be the dirt that we can pick up with our hands or plant flowers in. If we think of the priesthood solely in terms of the power and authority of God delegated to man—or the dirt in the Renlunds' analogy—we will find that we have been very narrow in our definition, leaving out much of God's power

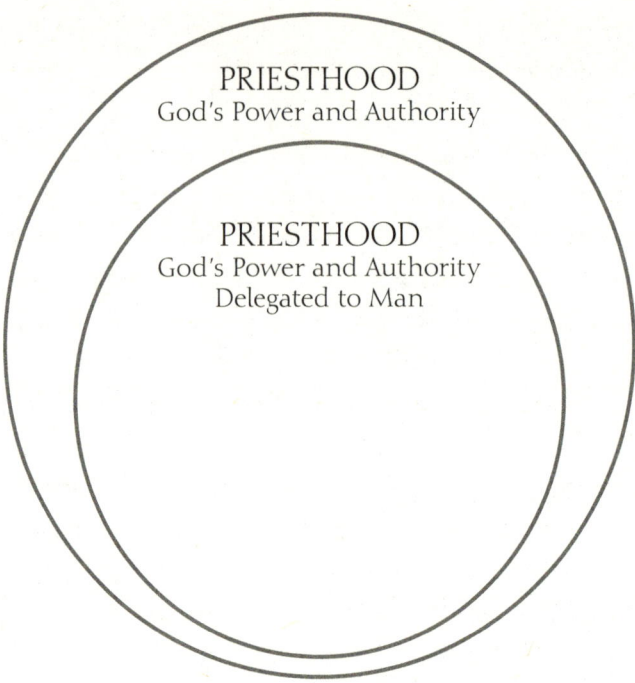

and authority. If we think of priesthood as the power and authority of God—or the entire globe in the Renlunds' analogy—we expand our view and include not only that which is commonly focused on but all that God defines as His power and authority.

In addition, over the history of the earth, the Lord has used two primary structures, frameworks, or governments in which the priesthood is administered: hierarchical/ecclesiastical and patriarchal/familial. During the time of Adam and Eve and throughout the Old Testament, the structure of priesthood government was patriarchal/familial. During the time of Christ and the beginning of the Restoration, however, the ecclesiastical or hierarchical structure that we are more familiar with today was introduced. During our dispensation, both the hierarchical and patriarchal/familial government structures have been in use. The hierarchical structure governs the priesthood used primarily in Church and is thus more public. The patriarchal/familial structure is used primarily in the more private and sacred settings of the temple and home. President Dallin H. Oaks affirmed, "A most important difference in the functioning of priesthood authority in the family and in the Church results from the fact that the government of the family is patriarchal, whereas the government of the Church is hierarchical."[7] The priesthood itself is not different—what varies is simply how the Lord has set up its system of governance. Both of these two systems of priesthood government will be described in detail later in this book.

It can be confusing! First, there are the differences between the overall priesthood power and authority of God and the priesthood power and authority that God has delegated to mankind. Then, there are also differences between the two priesthood government structures of this delegated power and authority. This confusion is enhanced with regard to women, as the priesthood applies to them differently in each setting. For example, many women who enter the temple wonder what it means for them to be endowed with priesthood power when they are told that only men hold the priesthood. Some women want to better understand how to use priesthood authority in their Church callings, as President Oaks instructed, but are still being told that they don't really have priesthood authority. Some women are told that through the endowment they have priesthood power in their homes, but they are also told that without the presence of a man there is no priesthood.

Perhaps a well-known parable could help clarify this confusion.

> It was six men of Indostan
> To learning much inclined,
> Who went to see the Elephant
> (Though all of them were blind),
> That each by observation
> Might satisfy his mind.

As each of the six blind men touches a different part of the elephant, he describes what he has discovered. One grabs a leg and describes the elephant as rough and round like a tree. The second analyzes the tusk and describes it as a spear. The third holds the tail and compares it to a rope. The fourth, thinking he is holding a snake, is actually describing the trunk.

The fascinating part of the parable is that they are all right to a certain extent, but, in their insistence on being right, they are also leaving many things unknown. In conclusion, the author writes:

And so these men of Indostan
Disputed loud and long,
Each in his own opinion
Exceeding stiff and strong,
Though each was partly in the right,
And all were in the wrong![8]

All of us have been in circumstances in which we knew for sure something was right, but realized later that perhaps we were looking "through a glass, darkly" (1 Corinthians 13:12).

In many ways, trying to understand the priesthood is similar. Let's say, for example, using the above analogy, that the priesthood is the entire elephant, and the different parts of the elephant are different aspects of the priesthood. Some see only the trunk of the elephant and call it "the priesthood," but they are really talking only about the men who are ordained to offices in the priesthood. Although that terminology is correct, it is only partially correct. Many are so accustomed to looking only at the trunk of the elephant that they forget, or have never realized, that they are not seeing the entire elephant. They may even correct others for being misguided. A woman, for example, can go to the temple and receive her endowment and believe she possesses priesthood power and authority, and correctly so. Although not ordained to a priesthood office, she has received this priesthood power and authority through the ordinances of the temple. The one holding the trunk of the elephant may correct her, stating that only men hold the priesthood, not realizing that she is talking

> The priesthood is much more than how God's power and authority is used in the hierarchical structure of the Church, and it is more than the power and authority of the patriarchal or familial structure given to both men and women in the temple.

about a different priesthood government structure altogether—a different part of the elephant, so to speak. They are actually both right! The priesthood is much more than how God's power and authority is used in the hierarchical structure of the Church, and it is more than the power and authority of the patriarchal or familial structure given to both men and women in the temple.

In its most holistic sense, priesthood is the power of God. The priesthood is to be used in order to help God's children return to Him and become like Him. Within the context of the greater priesthood, there are many powers, some called priesthood and others simply called powers, that exist for the same purpose. Sister Julie B. Beck, while instructing the women of the Church regarding the priesthood, differentiated between God's total priesthood power and authority, and that priesthood delegated to man. She declared, "We need never confuse the idea of those who hold the priesthood in trust, with the priesthood. The priesthood is God's power. It is His power to create, to bless, to lead, to serve as He does. . . . Don't confuse the power with the keys and the offices of the priesthood. God's power is limitless and it is shared with those who make and keep covenants. Too much is said and misunderstood about what the brothers have and the sisters don't have. This is Satan's way of confusing both men and women so neither understands what they really have."[9]

## THE PRIESTHOOD AND THE PLAN

When teaching significant points of doctrine, such as those related to the priesthood, I find it invaluable to put those points in the context of the plan of salvation. In so doing here, I will include many prophetic statements in order to ensure doctrinal accuracy on such an important and sensitive issue.

We understand that in the premortal realm we lived with our Heavenly Parents and desired to become like Them. Many Church leaders in our dispensation have instructed us on the importance of understanding that we have both a Heavenly Father and Mother and that They were married. When Elder Erastus Snow, for example, was asked the question, "Do you mean we should understand that Deity consists of man and woman?" he responded, "Most certainly I do. If I believe anything that

God has ever said about himself, . . . I must believe that Deity consists of man and woman. . . . There can be no God except he is composed of the man and woman united, and there is not in all the eternities that exist, nor ever will be, a God in any other way."[10] As our Heavenly Parents are married and have a family, we too must be sealed for eternity as husband and wife in order to have eternal life like Them. In fact, as President Dallin H. Oaks stated, "Our theology begins with heavenly parents. Our highest aspiration is to be like them."[11]

For years it seemed that the topic of Heavenly Mother was almost taboo. It is important to recognize, however, that never has a member of the Quorum of the Twelve or a prophet taught officially that we should not speak of a Heavenly Mother. In fact, over the years, the opposite has occurred. President Harold B. Lee confirmed this truth when he explained the divine parentage of Jesus Christ: "That great hymn 'O My Father' puts it correctly when Eliza R. Snow wrote, 'In the heav'ns are parents single? No, the thought makes reason stare! Truth is reason; truth eternal tells me I've a mother there.' Born of a Heavenly Mother, sired by a Heavenly Father, we knew Him, we were in His house."[12]

This idea of having a Heavenly Father and a Heavenly Mother is extremely important in completely understanding the plan of salvation. In fact, President M. Russell Ballard, in discussing a number of important gospel topics our youth should be familiar with, mentioned Heavenly Mother as one that teachers of the youth should know like the back of their hands.[13] I ask all my BYU students enrolled in "The Eternal Family," the required cornerstone class at Church schools: "Of all the doctrines and teachings that stood out to you in the class, what was most impactful?" Without fail, every semester, the majority of the female students respond that it is the truth and knowledge and open conversation regarding the reality of a Heavenly Mother. One of the quotes we use in class comes from Elder John A. Widtsoe, who confirmed, "This glorious vision of life hereafter . . . is given radiant warmth by the thought that . . . we shall find a mother who possesses the attributes of Godhood."[14]

The reality of having both a Heavenly Father and a Heavenly Mother is critical in this discussion regarding priesthood and the plan, in that it teaches us who we are and who we have the potential to become. Elder

Glenn L. Pace of the Seventy testified to the sisters of the Church that "when you stand in front of your heavenly parents in those royal courts on high and you look into Her eyes and behold Her countenance, any question you ever had about the role of women in the kingdom will evaporate into the rich celestial air, because at that moment you will see standing directly in front of you, your divine nature and destiny."[15]

In addition to understanding our divine heritage, it is also critical that we understand our potential in terms of family. President Nelson taught that "Priesthood authority has been restored so that families can be sealed eternally."[16] President Oaks added, "The theology of The Church of Jesus Christ of Latter-day Saints centers on the family. Our relationship to God and the purpose of earth life are explained in terms of the family. We are the spirit children of heavenly parents. The gospel plan is implemented through earthly families, and our highest aspiration is to perpetuate those family relationships throughout eternity. The ultimate mission of our Savior's Church is to help us achieve exaltation in the celestial kingdom, and that can only be accomplished in a family relationship."[17]

The priesthood organization used in the eternal family is patriarchal/familial. Robert Millet, former dean of Religious Education at Brigham Young University and well-respected Latter-day Saint theologian, taught: "The patriarchal order was established by God and predates mortal institutions. Our God is also our Father, our Father in heaven. He is a man, a glorified, resurrected man, a Man of Holiness (Moses 6:57).... God lives in the family unit.... In the premortal existence—our first estate—we lived under the patriarchal order, the family order. It was an order consisting of Father, Mother, and children, an order presided over by our Parents and directed by love, kindness, gentleness, and godly persuasion. We are thus children of God, members of the royal family. Our souls are eternally attuned and acclimated to family things."[18]

As members of The Church of Jesus Christ of Latter-day Saints, we have been taught, we understand, and we teach that we are part of a heavenly family. "I Am a Child of God" is one of the first songs we learn as Primary children, and we sing it throughout our lives. The family proclamation teaches: "All human beings—male and female—are created in the image of God. Each is a beloved spirit son or daughter of heavenly parents, and, as such, each has a divine nature and destiny.... In the premortal realm, spirit sons and daughters knew and worshipped God as their Eternal Father and accepted His plan by which His children could obtain a physical body and gain earthly experience to progress toward perfection and ultimately realize their divine destiny as heirs of eternal life."[19]

We also believe that our Heavenly Parents once lived as we do now, and that if we follow Their pattern, we will return to live with Them and become like Them. The Prophet Joseph Smith taught that "God Himself was once as we are now, and is an exalted man, and sits enthroned in yonder heavens! That is the great secret. If the veil were rent today, and the great God who holds this world in its orbit, and who upholds all worlds and all things by His power, was to make Himself visible, I say, if you were to see Him today, you would see Him like a man in form—like yourselves in all the person, image, and very form as a man; for Adam was created in the very fashion, image and likeness of God, and received instruction from, and walked, talked and conversed with Him, as one man talks and communes with another."[20]

Our Heavenly Parents not only lived as we once did, but They too, according to the laws of God, made and kept sacred covenants in order to become what They are today. Just as we do, They too made and kept sacred temple covenants as part of Their preparation to enter into the eternal patriarchal/family order of the priesthood.[21] President Wilford Woodruff taught that the Lord "has had His endowments long ago; it is thousands and millions of years since He received His blessings."[22] Brigham Young taught the pattern for becoming Gods. He instructed, "After men have got their exaltations and their crowns—have become Gods, even the sons of God—are made Kings of kings and Lords of lords, they have the power then of propagating their species in spirit; and that is the first of their operations with regard to organizing a world."[23] It is impossible, however, for a man to reign as a God and propagate his species without a wife, a Goddess who, by his side, in their family/patriarchal order, rules and reigns together with him.

In his beautiful, literate style, Elder James E. Talmage taught the reality of our divine nature and future, following the pattern of our Heavenly

Parents: "In the glorified state of the blessed hereafter, husband and wife will administer in their respective stations, seeing and understanding alike, and co-operating to the full in the government of their family kingdom.... Then shall woman reign by Divine right, a queen in the resplendent realm of her glorified state, even as exalted man shall stand, priest and king unto the Most High God. Mortal eye cannot see nor mind comprehend the beauty, glory, and majesty of a righteous woman made perfect in the celestial kingdom of God."[24]

The reality that we have Heavenly Parents, that we are Their children, and that we have potential to become like Them is the core of what we as members of the Church believe. In fact, our divine potential—which seems blasphemous to some, but is sacred, inspiring, and true to us—is the greatest motivating factor to follow the commandments of God, make sacred covenants, keep them, and teach them to our families and the world. It was this very truth that motivated us to leave our premortal innocent and secure state with our heavenly family and come to this earth as children of God but veiled from Their presence. We recognized the joy, the happiness, and the love of our Heavenly Parents. We desired to be like Them and knew that only through eternal marriage covenants could that be possible.

Through the plan of salvation, centered in the Atonement of Jesus Christ and possible only through Him, we are as individuals able to return and become like our Heavenly Parents, to live eternally with and like Them. Only through the sacred covenants made available through the priesthood are we able to participate in the ordinances required for this to happen. Thus, starting with our first parents, the priesthood, organized in the earliest dispensation through the eternal order of God, the family/patriarchal order, was taught and made available on the earth.

## PATRIARCHAL ORDER OF THE PRIESTHOOD FROM ADAM AND EVE TO ABRAHAM

After Adam and Eve were created "in the image of the Gods" (Abraham 4:27), they were placed on earth and were privileged to walk and talk with God. Their goal was to become like our Heavenly Parents. In fact, their goal was to be able to have an eternal family like that of

Heavenly Father and Heavenly Mother. Joseph Smith taught that Adam and Eve were married in the Garden of Eden.[25] However, there was still more to be done. In order for Eve and Adam to progress, they would have to perform an act that would ultimately require the Atonement of Jesus Christ, thus putting Christ at the center of mortality. President Henry B. Eyring taught, "It was Eve who received the knowledge that Adam needed to partake of the fruit of the tree of knowledge for them to keep all of God's commandments and to form a family,"[26] and Adam was wise enough to join her. They were brought into mortality, no longer able to enjoy the constant presence of the Father.

Knowing that it was their desire to return to His presence and become like Him, and for their posterity to have the same blessing, God the Father provided a way for Adam and Eve to return to their Heavenly Parents. This "plan of salvation" required the willing sacrifice of the innocent blood of the "Only Begotten" and perfect Son of God (Moses 6:62). Through His perfect Atonement, Jesus Christ made it possible for Adam and Eve and all of their posterity to return to the presence of God and live forever.

Thus, in order for Adam and Eve and all of their posterity, including us, to return to the presence of our Heavenly Parents, two things were necessary. The first was Christ's atoning sacrifice, which overcame physical and spiritual death. Second was the making and keeping of sacred covenants through receiving ordinances, including baptism, conferral of the Holy Ghost, priesthood ordination for men, and the endowment and sealing for men and women alike. According to the Prophet Joseph Smith, "Adam blessed his posterity" because "he wanted to bring them into the presence of God."[27]

Adam not only blessed his posterity, but he and Eve and their righteous posterity were baptized and received the Holy Ghost, and Adam was ordained to the priesthood (Moses 6:51–68). Eventually they would individually also make sacred priesthood covenants with God, including all that today happens in the temple, and together they entered into what we now call the patriarchal order of the priesthood. "This order [meaning the patriarchal order of the priesthood as found only in the temple today] was instituted in the days of Adam, and came down by lineage . . . that his posterity should be the chosen of the Lord, and that they should be preserved unto the end of the earth" (Doctrine and Covenants 107:41–42).

Regarding the patriarchal order of the priesthood and temple, President Ezra Taft Benson taught: "Adam and his posterity were commanded by God to be baptized, to receive the Holy Ghost, and to enter into the order of the Son of God. To enter into the order of the Son of God is the equivalent today of entering into the fulness of the Melchizedek Priesthood, which is only received in the house of the Lord. Because Adam and Eve had complied with these requirements, God said to them, 'Thou art after the order of him who was without beginning of days or end of years, from all eternity to all eternity.' (Moses 6:67.)"[28]

> It is perhaps ironic that the priesthood government structure named *patriarchal* was absolutely dependent equally on both men as patriarchs and women as matriarchs.

This patriarchal or family order of the Melchizedek Priesthood continued throughout the Old Testament, with husbands and wives making covenants together with the Lord, and both men and women receiving sacred priesthood ordinances. In fact, it is perhaps ironic that the priesthood government structure named *patriarchal* was absolutely dependent equally on both men as patriarchs and women as matriarchs. Thus, it is significant that President Benson spoke of it as "an order of family government."[29] President Russell M. Nelson clarified that "Adam held the priesthood, and Eve served in matriarchal partnership with the patriarchal priesthood."[30] This patriarchal order of the priesthood was entered into by Enoch and his wife, who brought their family into the presence of God as the result of making and keeping covenants with the Lord and becoming a Christlike people.[31]

Noah and Shem and their wives followed the same pattern after the flood, and it continued with Abraham and Sarah, the great patriarch and matriarch. It is because of Abraham and Sarah's righteousness that they, along with all covenant-making members of the Church, will be blessed with all of the blessings of the Abrahamic covenant. It was through the loins and influence of both Abraham and Sarah that Isaac was born and raised unto God (see Genesis 21:12). Of Isaac's wife, Rebekah, Elder Bruce R. McConkie related, "I think Rebekah is one of the greatest patterns in all the revelations of what a woman can do to influence a family in righteousness." He continued, "Women are appointed, like Rebekah, to be guides and lights in righteousness in the family unit, and to engineer and arrange so that things are done in the way that will result in the salvation of more of our Father's children." It was to Rebekah, not Isaac, Elder McConkie explained, that the Lord revealed "the destiny of nations that are to be born that are yet in your womb."[32] In fact, it was Rebekah's younger son, whose name was changed by God to Israel, who became the father of the house of Israel.

Thus, all who fully enter into covenants with the Lord, including that of the patriarchal/familial order, are taking part in the gathering of the house of Israel. The house of Israel therefore becomes a symbol—or perhaps even stronger, a foreshadow—of the eternal family of our Heavenly Parents. Robert Millet surmised that the "patriarchal order is a family order, a partnership, a joint stewardship. It is an eternal principle—the man and the woman are not alone: neither is the man without the woman, nor the woman without the man in the Lord."[33]

Elder Bruce R. McConkie taught that "the government the Lord gave him [Adam] was patriarchal" and that "this theocratic system, patterned after the order and system that prevailed in heaven, was the government of God. He himself, though dwelling in heaven, was the Lawgiver, Judge, and King. He gave direction in all things both civil and ecclesiastical; there was no separation of church and state as we now know it. All governmental affairs were directed, controlled, and regulated from on high. The Lord's legal administrators on earth served by virtue of their callings and ordinations in the Holy Priesthood and as they were guided by the power of the Holy Ghost."[34]

## PATRIARCHAL ORDER OF THE PRIESTHOOD FROM MOSES TO ELIJAH

This order of priesthood government continued from Adam to Moses. In fact, Moses also lived and taught this order of the priesthood to his people and "sought diligently to sanctify his people that they might behold the face of God" (Doctrine and Covenants 84:23). We would assume, therefore, that Moses not only performed the ordinances of baptism and the conferral of the Holy Ghost, but also taught his people about the temple. Exodus 40:12–13 teaches us that God instructed Moses: "Thou shalt bring Aaron and his sons unto the door of the tabernacle of the congregation, and wash them with water. And thou shalt put upon Aaron the holy garments, and anoint him, and sanctify him."

Doctrine and Covenants 84, a section referring to the patriarchal order of the priesthood and the temple, teaches us, however, that during the time of Moses, these covenant-making members "hardened their hearts and could not endure his presence; therefore, the Lord in his wrath, for his anger was kindled against them, swore that they should not enter into his rest while in the wilderness, which rest is the fulness of his glory. Therefore, he took Moses out of their midst, and the Holy Priesthood also" (vv. 24–25).

Moses and his people had the patriarchal order of the priesthood, but because of their unrighteousness, this order of the priesthood was taken away. We learn from Joseph Smith that the Lord further instructed Moses, "I will take away the priesthood out of their midst; therefore my holy order, and the ordinances thereof" (JST, Exodus 34:1). The governing priesthood became the Aaronic Priesthood, or preparatory priesthood, for this period of time, allowing ordinances such as baptism to take place. But, with rare exception, no ordinances of the patriarchal order of the priesthood were performed (see Doctrine and Covenants 84:19–27). President Benson taught, "This higher priesthood, with its attendant ordinances, was taken from Israel till the time of Jesus Christ. . . . Between Moses and Christ only certain prophets possessed the right to the higher priesthood and the blessings that could bring men into the presence of God. One of these prophets was Elijah."[35]

Elijah has made it possible for all those willing to make and keep covenants with the Lord pertaining to the patriarchal order of the priesthood to be sealed with their families forever and to be given all that the Father has (see Doctrine and Covenants 110:13–14). Elijah was translated at the end of his life, allowing him to physically restore the keys of the priesthood in the future to Peter, James, and John on the Mount of Transfiguration. Later, in our own dispensation, Elijah, now a resurrected being (see D&C 133:54–55), restored that same authority to Joseph Smith and Oliver Cowdery in the Kirtland Temple in April 1836.

## HIERARCHICAL PRIESTHOOD FROM CHRIST'S MORTAL MINISTRY THROUGH THE APOSTASY

During His mortal ministry Jesus established His Church, an ecclesiastical/hierarchical structure, so that, according to Elder McConkie, the Church could operate in the "easiest and [most] harmonious way because of the social setting that exists in the world. And the social circumstances of the nations and the governments are such today that we can't operate through families like they did in Abraham's day. You can't have civil and ecclesiastical authority combined because the great masses of men don't belong to the Church."[36] The organizational structure of the Church therefore went from patriarchal/familial to hierarchical/ecclesiastical. The doctrine of the priesthood did not change, but the application, procedures, and policies of how the Lord structured His priesthood did change, primarily in the public setting.

It is important to note, however, that during the time of Christ, even though the main priesthood functioned in the hierarchical Church structure, while on the Mount of Transfiguration, Peter, James, and John received their endowments as well as the keys of the higher priesthood from Moses, Elijah, and other heavenly messengers (see Matthew 17:1–9; 2 Peter 1:16–18).[37] We would presume, therefore, the patriarchal order was put into place on the earth, allowing for the sealing ordinance, although the hierarchical/ecclesiastical structure remained in place as it is today.

This new hierarchical Church structure along with the keys of the patriarchal priesthood did not exist for long, however, because as Christ and the Apostles were killed, the keys of the Melchizedek Priesthood were taken away. "Even before the early Apostles completed their labors,"

President Nelson explained, "the Apostasy began. It occurred, as prophesied, when teachings of men with priesthood keys were rejected and sacred ordinances were defiled."[38] For over a thousand years, neither the hierarchical/ecclesiastical nor the patriarchal/familial structure of God's priesthood government existed on the earth.

It is crucial to note that although no one on the earth held these priesthood keys during this time of apostasy,[39] either in the patriarchal or hierarchical priesthood, the larger priesthood, or the power and authority of God, was still available. Elder and Sister Renlund explained: "Even after the Great Apostasy, God was not 'snoozing' until the priesthood was conferred on Joseph Smith and Oliver Cowdery on May 15, 1829 (Doctrine and Covenants 13). Before and after the Reformation, God blessed men and women, Protestants, Catholics, and non-Christians by His priesthood power and authority as they prayed and lived according to the light and knowledge they received."[40] In fact, in 1820, even before the priesthood was restored, Joseph Smith as a youth received the visitation of the Father and the Son and accessed God's priesthood power. He translated the entire Book of Mormon before the priesthood was even restored.[41]

## HIERARCHICAL AND PATRIARCHAL/FAMILY PRIESTHOOD FROM THE RESTORATION TO TODAY

As the Prophet Joseph Smith taught, "The keys have to be brought from heaven whenever the Gospel is sent."[42] Thus, in 1820, in answer to Joseph's heartfelt prayer, God the Father and his Son Jesus Christ appeared to the young man. Almost a decade later, the Aaronic and Melchizedek Priesthoods were restored, followed by the organization of the Church in 1830, and the calling and organizing of the first high priests, First Presidency, Quorum of the Twelve Apostles, and Seventy within the next five years. Through a line-upon-line process, God once again instituted the hierarchical structure of the Church. Before Joseph's martyrdom, the Relief Society was necessarily restored as well.

As early as 1823, however, Joseph was promised by the Lord, through Moroni, "I will reveal unto you the Priesthood, by the hand of Elijah the prophet, before the coming of the great and dreadful day of the Lord.

... And he shall plant in the hearts of the children the promises made to the fathers, and the hearts of the children shall turn to their fathers. If it were not so," came the enlightening explanation of the Lord, "the whole earth would be utterly wasted at his coming" (Joseph Smith—History 1:38–39). Although the Church had been restored and the Aaronic and Melchizedek Priesthoods organized in the hierarchical government structure, Moroni's promise was not yet fulfilled.

Finally, on April 3, 1836, in the Kirtland Temple, Jesus Christ returned as promised, and Moses, Elias, and Elijah came to reveal additional priesthood responsibilities that would fulfill Moroni's promise. Moses delivered the keys of the gathering of Israel (see Doctrine and Covenants 110:11); Elias, the keys of the Abrahamic covenant (see v. 12); and Elijah, the keys of the sealing authority (see Doctrine and Covenants 27:9; 110:13–16; see also 128:17–18, 21; 132:7, 19).[43]

Why did the Lord send Elijah? According to Joseph Smith, "Because he holds the keys of the authority to administer in all the ordinances of the Priesthood."[44] Joseph also instructed that these keys were "the revelation, ordinances, oracles, powers and endowments of the fulness of the Melchizedek Priesthood and of the kingdom of God on the earth."[45] Now, note the critical sequence of the receiving of these priesthoods, according to President Benson, "Even though the Aaronic Priesthood and Melchizedek Priesthood had been restored to the earth, the Lord urged the Saints to build a temple to receive the keys by which *this order* of priesthood could be administered on the earth again, 'for there [was] not a place found on earth that he may come to and restore again that which was lost ... *even the fulness of the priesthood*' (D&C 124:28; italics added)."[46] Joseph Smith taught, "If a man gets a fulness of the priesthood of God, he has to get it in the same way that Jesus Christ obtained it, and that was by keeping all the commandments and obeying all the ordinances of the house of the Lord."[47] Hence the need for the Kirtland Temple and the keys of the fulness of the priesthood revealed by Elijah.

Thus, in the final dispensation, "a whole and complete and perfect union, and welding together of dispensations, and keys, and powers, and glories should take place, and be revealed from the days of Adam even to the present time" (Doctrine and Covenants 128:18). During Joseph

Smith's tenure as prophet, both the hierarchical and patriarchal priesthood structures were apparent. It seems as if Joseph was trying to learn from the Lord both how to structure a Church, using the hierarchical priesthood structure, and how to create Zion and prepare the members for eternal life as promised in the temple, using the patriarchal structure of the priesthood. In other words, during Joseph's leadership, the hierarchical structure used in the public Church organization (with Apostles, prophets, seventy, and so on) and the familial or patriarchal structure used in the temple (with men and women receiving the power and authority associated with the patriarchal order of the priesthood) were not only both being used, but they were dependent upon each other. Joseph was evidently receiving revelation from the Lord regarding both priesthood structures simultaneously.

It is important to recognize that today we need the hierarchical structure of the Church and the authority and keys of those who hold the Melchizedek Priesthood in order for the patriarchal priesthood to have effect. Note that although there are two structures within the larger priesthood context, these two overlap and are dependent on each other. For example, the prophet is the great high priest on earth over both, using the keys Jesus Christ gave him for the salvation of mankind. One must receive from an ordained priesthood holder the ordinances performed outside of the temple, baptism and confirmation of the Holy Ghost, in order to receive further ordinances inside the temple. It is, however, important to note that just because a man has been ordained to the Melchizedek Priesthood, which gives him the power to perform all ordinances in the Church and to enter the temple, that ordination does not give him the *authority* to perform ordinances that pertain only to the temple, including the initiatory, endowment, and sealing. Thus, only men are authorized to perform priesthood ordinances outside of the temple, but both men and women are authorized to perform certain ordinances in the temple.

In the following diagram, the larger circle represents God's total priesthood, meaning His power and authority. The inner circle represents God's priesthood that He has delegated to His children on earth. The two overlapping circles inside the smaller circle represent the two government structures the Lord has instituted since the days of Adam and Eve,

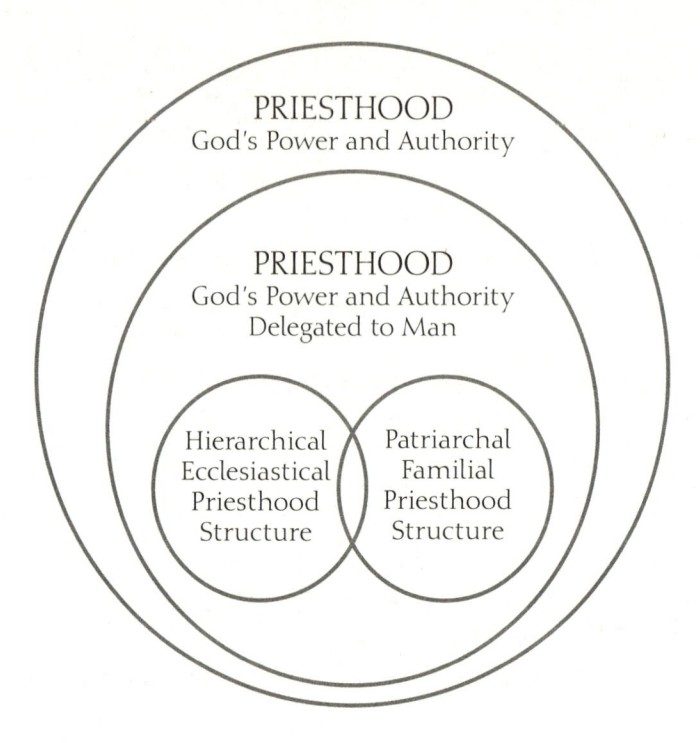

```
          PRIESTHOOD
      God's Power and Authority

          PRIESTHOOD
      God's Power and Authority
         Delegated to Man

    Hierarchical    Patriarchal
   Ecclesiastical    Familial
    Priesthood     Priesthood
     Structure      Structure
```

namely the hierarchical/ecclesiastical and the patriarchal/familial. The ordinances and covenants of the gospel of Jesus Christ are represented in the overlapping part of the circles.

It is also important to remember that although in mortality the two priesthood government systems overlap, in the eternities, it will be the fulness of the priesthood—the patriarchal or familial system of the priesthood—that will continue, with all the keys, ordinances, and privileges necessary for eternal life encapsulated into this one priesthood system. In other words, what really matters, and what is eternally important, is the family, and therefore, we see a renewed emphasis on the role of women and the family in our day.

To this end, President Ballard taught: "Although the Church plays a pivotal role in proclaiming, announcing, and administering the necessary ordinances of salvation and exaltation, all of that, as important as it is, is really just the scaffolding being used in an infinite and eternal construction project to build, support, and strengthen the family. And just as scaffolding is eventually taken down and put away to reveal the final completed building, so too will the mortal, administrative functions of the Church eventually fade as the eternal family comes fully into view. In that context, it's important to remember that our Church assignments are only temporary, and that at some point we will all be released either by our leaders or by death. But we will never be released from our eternal callings within the family."[48]

Although the Church and family support each other, and both are dependent on each other, that which will remain is the family. "Every law and principle and power, every belief, every ordinance and ordination, every covenant, every sermon and every sacrament, every counsel and correction, the sealings, the calls, the releases, the service," according to President Boyd K. Packer, "have as their ultimate purpose the perfection of the individual and the family."[49]

## CONCLUSION

I've often thought how different our understanding of the priesthood would be, especially as women, if the emphasis of the leaders of the Church were on the family rather than on the Church. What might happen if we focused more on the patriarchal/familial structure of the priesthood rather than on the hierarchical/ecclesiastical system when discussing the priesthood in leadership training, in our various meetings, and in our gospel-related classes? How different would things be if we as members of the Church focused more on the family and the order entered into by Eve and Adam, Sarah and Abraham, Rebekah and Isaac, even Heavenly Mother and Heavenly Father? How different would it be if we truly realized that

> How different would things be if we as members of the Church focused more on the family and the order entered into by Eve and Adam, Sarah and Abraham, Rebekah and Isaac, even Heavenly Mother and Heavenly Father?

the temporary hierarchical structure of the Church is meant to support the familial/patriarchal structure of the eternal family?

I imagine that we would see priesthood more in terms of how it relates to the family. We would be likelier to recognize the critical role of women, and how both men and women really do work together "to bring to pass the immortality and eternal life of man" (Moses 1:39), as demonstrated by President Kimball and my parents. We would realize that women who have been endowed with priesthood power in the temple have priesthood in their own lives and in the lives of their family members, and that the priesthood resides in their homes, regardless of their marital status or their husbands' activity level. Perhaps we would begin to comprehend in part, as taught by President Russell M. Nelson, that "all the purposes of the world and all that was in the world would be brought to naught without woman—a keystone in the priesthood arch of creation."[50]

In our day, the Lord, through His divinely appointed prophets, is teaching these concepts in their fulness. Our Church leaders are emphasizing the eternal, familial/patriarchal structure of priesthood government, along with the important role of the hierarchical/ecclesiastical structure of priesthood government to assist in the building of eternal families. In so doing, the Lord, through His prophets and leaders, is guiding and directing and pleading with the women of the Church to take their needful and rightful places in the family alongside the men. Women are being taught the importance of having direct access to God; they are learning their divine role in His plan. By accepting and acting upon the invitations, pleas, and admonitions of God's chosen servants, both women and men together will be blessed to receive all that we desired and were promised by our Heavenly Parents in our premortal realm.

Chapter 2

# PRIESTHOOD KEYS, AUTHORITY, AND POWER IN THE CHURCH

Only months before I left on my mission, my family gathered together under the direction of my father, and he offered a family prayer in behalf of my oldest sister, who had been diagnosed with breast cancer and given only six months to live. He laid his hands upon my sister's head and, by the authority of the Melchizedek Priesthood that he held, blessed her that her life would be saved. And it was.

I remember lying by my mother's side in bed after she found out that she had brain cancer and pleading and wishing that she would be given the blessing to live. That blessing was never given. I do, however, remember the sweet and tender priesthood blessings given to her that she would be strong and full of courage and faith until the end of her life. And she was.

I have been blessed by an incredible father, husband, ministering brethren, friends, brothers, and other men who hold and use the priesthood in a variety of ways. I am forever grateful for those who hold and are worthy of the authority of the priesthood here on the earth, and who act under the direction of those who hold priesthood keys. I've seen the power of the priesthood exercised in many ways throughout my life, and I know it is real. I believe you do as well. I am grateful to the Lord for establishing a Church in a hierarchical structure that allows worthy men to be ordained to offices of the priesthood and exercise His power and authority on earth. In fact, if there were a line of people standing to testify of the blessings associated with those who hold offices of the priesthood and perform ordinances and assignments associated with their offices, including baptism, the sacrament, father's blessings, patriarchal blessings, receiving the gift of the Holy Ghost, temple endowment, sealings, and so on, I would push to be at the head of the line.

In addition, I have a firm testimony of prophets and apostles on the earth today, their divine role as witnesses of Jesus Christ, and the keys, power, and authority they possess. I sustain them unequivocally. I am fascinated with their attention to seniority and their love for each other as members of the Quorum of the Twelve Apostles and First Presidency. I love how they treat and respect their spouses and families. Most important, I appreciate their special witness of Jesus Christ and believe they speak for Him today. Like Enoch the seer, they see "things which [are] not visible to the natural eye" (Moses 6:36).

In short, I have a testimony of and appreciation for the hierarchical priesthood. But, in a landmark address given over a decade ago in general conference, entitled "Priesthood Authority in the Family and in the Church," President Dallin H. Oaks explained that priesthood functions differently in the family from the way it does in the Church. That talk has helped delineate significant differences between the hierarchical and patriarchal priesthood structures. To demonstrate those similarities and differences, President Oaks used the following story:

"My father died when I was seven. I was the oldest of three small children our widowed mother struggled to raise. When I was ordained a deacon, she said how pleased she was to have a priesthood holder in the home. But Mother continued to direct the family, including calling on which one of us would pray when we knelt together each morning. I was puzzled. I had been taught that the priesthood presided in the family. There must be something I didn't know about how that principle worked." Many, like President Oaks was as a youth, are "puzzled" by how the priesthood functions in the Church administration and in the family, perhaps because, as acknowledged by President Oaks, "it is rarely explained."[1]

After sharing this experience of President Oaks with my students, I often ask how many of them were raised in homes where their mother, if single, or when the father was gone, called upon a brother to pick someone to pray "because he held the priesthood." Or, when the father was gone, a brother, rather than the mother, took charge of family scripture study and prayer, making sure it happened, as if he were the presiding figure. Without fail, around half of the students who were themselves the brother, or who had a brother in the home who held the priesthood, responded in the affirmative. Many young women especially have shared that they were bothered by that, but never understood why.

In this chapter, we will strive to develop doctrinal foundation regarding priesthood authority, priesthood keys, and priesthood power in the hierarchical structure of the Church as taught by God through ancient and modern prophets. We will use this foundation to better understand how priesthood applies to women at church specifically in chapter 3 and women in the temple and family in chapters 4 and 5.

## PRIESTHOOD AUTHORITY IN THE CHURCH

In order to become like our Heavenly Parents and to live with Them for eternity, all of us needed the opportunity to have a mortal body and to experience life through the exercise of faith, and thus we needed to be out of Their presence. Although God's plan was perfect, we, His children, were not perfect. We did not have the power and authority within us to save ourselves; we could not return to live with and become like our Heavenly Parents without Christ's Atonement. Because Christ fulfilled His saving Atonement, He has the power and authority to redeem all of our Heavenly Parents' children (see Alma 34:10–15). The power and authority that Christ possesses is called the priesthood (see Alma 13:7–8).

The overarching and ultimate purpose of the priesthood, therefore, is to make salvation and exaltation possible for all of God's children. Every time priesthood keys are used or a priesthood ordinance is performed, it is for the purpose of saving and exalting God's children. Christ delegated this priesthood to our Father's children on earth in order to help bring about this purpose. Those who hold priesthood keys of presidency, primarily apostolic keys, govern the use of this priesthood. These keys include

> The overarching and ultimate purpose of the priesthood . . . is to make salvation and exaltation possible for all of God's children.

the right of presidency, oversight, and directing power. Priesthood authority, then, is the permission granted by a priesthood key holder, someone who holds the key of presidency, to act in the name of Jesus Christ. Those who have priesthood authority act under the direction of the priesthood key holder when they provide blessings, teachings, and the ordinances and covenants necessary to gain salvation and eternal life. Priesthood authority in the hierarchical structure of the Church is received in two ways: through ordination and through being called and set apart.

## Priesthood Authority through Ordination

When the priesthood is conferred on a man, he is ordained to an office in the priesthood under the direction of one who holds the priesthood key of presidency over that individual. The offices in the Aaronic Priesthood are deacon, teacher, priest, and bishop. The offices of the Melchizedek Priesthood are elder, high priest, patriarch, Seventy, and Apostle. Each priesthood office carries duties and responsibilities. Each quorum is presided over by a quorum president, who teaches the members their duties and asks them to fill assignments. Some of the duties of a deacon are "to pass the sacrament to members of the Church, keep Church buildings and grounds in good order, act as messengers for priesthood leaders, and fulfill special assignments such as collecting fast offerings. . . . Elders are called to teach, expound, exhort, baptize, and watch over the Church (see D&C 20:42). . . . They have the authority to bestow the gift of the Holy Ghost by the laying on of hands (see D&C 20:43). . . . Elders may administer to the sick (see D&C 42:44) and bless little children (see D&C 20:70)."[2] It is important to note that, for the most part, priesthood authority that comes through ordination authorizes men to perform sacred ordinances, but the recipients of these ordinances are both men and women.

## Priesthood Authority through Being Called and Set Apart

Another way for an individual to receive priesthood authority is by being called and set apart under the authority of one who holds the priesthood key of presidency. This second way has been clarified recently by senior members of the Quorum of the Twelve and First Presidency. President M. Russell Ballard opened the window for a wider understanding of who possesses priesthood authority in the Church. "Those who have priesthood keys . . . literally make it possible for all who serve faithfully under their direction to exercise priesthood authority and have access to priesthood power."[3]

President Oaks elucidated the role of women in regard to the priesthood in the hierarchical Church: "We are not accustomed to speaking of women having the authority of the priesthood in their Church callings, but what other authority can it be? When a woman—young or old—is set apart to preach the gospel as a full-time missionary, she is given priesthood authority to perform a priesthood function." He continued, "The same is true when a woman is set apart to function as an officer or teacher in a Church organization under the direction of one who holds the keys of the priesthood. Whoever functions in an office or calling received from one who holds priesthood keys exercises priesthood authority in performing her or his assigned duties."[4] Priesthood authority, therefore, is given to both women and men, based on their callings.

## PRIESTHOOD KEYS

A few years ago, I asked my class of fifty Doctrine and Covenants students if they felt confident in their knowledge of the doctrine, principles, and practices associated with the priesthood. Apparently, all did! I was so happy at that moment, thinking that we would save several hours of class time on the topic. In the silence of my office following class, however, I began to wonder how likely it was that they knew everything about the priesthood when I myself, and even Church leaders, were struggling to understand and explain some of the fundamentals. During the next class, therefore, I had them answer the following on a slip of paper: "How many people in this room hold priesthood keys?"

I was surprised as I read aloud their diverse responses! "1," "50,"

"25," "4," "all of us," "none of us," "just the men in the room who hold the priesthood," "all who have been through the temple," and my favorite, most sincere answer, "I have no idea!" There were literally almost as many answers as there were students in that room. At least 75 percent of these students, men and women combined, were returned missionaries! I stood speechless for a moment, then realized that the hour I thought I had saved was now multiplied. Although they thought they had a good handle on the priesthood, they clearly did not know how much they were missing—and, therefore, what privileges they were not taking advantage of. (Throughout this book, we will look together to find the answers to the question I posed to the students as explained through the scriptures and modern-day prophets.)

After pondering upon the inability of my students to answer such a seemingly simple question, I went to one of my well-seasoned, mature, and wise colleagues in the Church history and doctrine department at BYU. I related the story of how my students didn't know the answer to what seemed like such a basic question, to which he humbly responded, "What keys were you referring to?" I stopped cold in my tracks. I realized immediately that not only did my students not understand, but I still was not grasping the full concept of priesthood keys, and perhaps there were more keys than I had previously thought.

Through my continued study of priesthood keys, it has become clear to me that, just as there are various parts to the elephant when it comes to the priesthood, there are also various parts of the elephant when referring to priesthood keys. Just as there is an all-encompassing priesthood and a smaller segment of the priesthood on earth, which we commonly refer to, the same is true with keys.

A closer look at the definition of priesthood keys in the Church's *Handbook 2: Administering the Church* helps us to understand this more clearly. The handbook states that "Jesus Christ holds all the keys of the priesthood pertaining to His Church," and that He "conferred upon each of His Apostles all the keys that pertain to the kingdom of God on earth" in this dispensation. "The senior living Apostle, the President of the Church, is the only person on earth authorized to exercise all priesthood keys.... The President of the Church delegates *priesthood keys* [typically known as the *keys of presidency*][5] to other priesthood leaders so they can preside in their areas of responsibility. . . . This presiding authority [or, in other words, the *keys of presidency*] is valid only for the designated responsibilities," for a specific time, "and within the geographic jurisdiction of each leader's calling. When priesthood leaders are released from their callings, they no longer hold the associated keys."[6]

The keys that are typically referred to in the Church—in the most common use of the term—would better be titled *priesthood keys of presidency*. In fact, these keys are so commonly discussed that we typically refer to them simply as *keys* or *priesthood keys*. These keys of presidency "are the authority God has given to priesthood leaders to direct, control, and govern the use of His priesthood on earth" for a specific time and over a specific location. "The exercise of priesthood authority is governed by those who hold its keys (see D&C 65:2; 81:2; 124:123)."[7] In Doctrine and Covenants 107:8–9, we read about the "right of presidency" associated with the Melchizedek Priesthood. This right of presidency is associated with the keys of the priesthood but is only a component.

Although there is a variety of uses of the term *key* in scriptures, listed below are the priesthood keys that are most common. These include: (1) keys bestowed upon the Apostles (otherwise known as keys of succession or apostolic keys), (2) priesthood keys of presidency, and (3) general priesthood keys. Let's define each of these a little more carefully.

## Priesthood Keys Bestowed upon the Apostles

As stated previously, "Jesus Christ holds all the keys of the priesthood pertaining to His Church. He has conferred upon each of His Apostles all the [priesthood] keys that pertain to the kingdom of God on earth. The senior living Apostle, the President of the Church, is the only person on earth authorized to exercise all priesthood keys (see D&C 43:1–4; 81:2; 107:64–67, 91–92; 132:7)."[8] These apostolic keys will be discussed in greater detail in chapter 5.

## Priesthood Keys of Presidency

"The President of the Church delegates priesthood keys to other priesthood leaders so they can preside in their areas of responsibility. Priesthood keys are bestowed on presidents of temples, missions, stakes, and districts;

bishops; branch presidents; and quorum presidents."[9] The authority received for each of these keys depends upon the assignment or calling of the individual. "Priesthood leaders who receive keys also are given the right to special gifts or power. . . . For example, a bishop serves as a common judge and receives the spiritual capacity to help members who need counsel with important personal problems, including serious transgressions."[10]

Those who hold priesthood keys of presidency may overlap in geographic boundaries but have different yet complementary authority. Often, these priesthood keys of presidency are similar, requiring each key holder to work carefully with other key holders in his area. A stake president, for example, has keys of presidency that authorize him to interview a couple and determine their worthiness to enter the temple to be sealed, but he does not have the authority to seal this couple, as the keys to seal belong to the Apostles and are delegated by them specifically to the temple sealers. Although there is some overlap in purposes, the authority of each of these keys is distinct.

When serving as the institute director in Boston, I worked closely with the stake president to help with activation and enrollment of young single adults within his geographic area. At the same time, I worked closely with the mission president to help young single adult investigators who came with the missionaries to be befriended and taught correct doctrine. As we tried to open a visitors' center to attract those who were not Latter-day Saints to the Longfellow Park building, the stake president, who held presiding priesthood keys for that function, had the authority to decide if the building was to be so used. As the institute director, with an occupational assignment (but not holding priesthood keys for this assignment), I helped coordinate the efforts of the young single adults according to class schedule, facilitated instruction, and gave suggestions to the stake president. The mission president, who held presiding priesthood keys for the missionaries in that geographic area, assigned missionaries certain nights to be available to answer investigators' questions. All three of us—two presiding priesthood key holders and one professional institute director—worked closely together for the benefit of the members and nonmembers in the area. (Perhaps it is worth saying that Church employees, such as someone in my position as an institute director, regardless of Church calling or priesthood responsibilities, do not hold priesthood authority as part of their work assignment. This has been confusing for some.)

This presiding authority as a priesthood key holder is limited to "the geographic jurisdiction of each leader's calling,"[11] and is delegated only for a specified period of time. "For example, a bishop serves as the presiding high priest in a ward and also as the president of the Aaronic Priesthood for the ward."[12] The bishop holds the priesthood keys of presidency and thus presides over all people living within his geographic jurisdiction, or ward boundary, for a period of time. Deacons quorum, teachers quorum, and elders quorum presidents hold the keys of presidency for the young men and men in their respective quorums for a specified period of time. "When priesthood leaders are released from their callings, they no longer hold the associated keys."[13]

Further: "All ward and stake auxiliary organizations operate under the direction of the bishop or stake president, who holds the keys to preside. Auxiliary presidents and their counselors [as well as counselors to priesthood leaders who hold the keys of presidency] do not receive keys. They receive delegated authority to function in their callings."[14]

## General Priesthood Keys Held by Priesthood Holders

"The general use of the term 'priesthood keys' or 'keys of the priesthood' can be understood as rights belonging to and available to priesthood leaders," but the blessings and privileges flowing from them also belong to all members of the Church who are worthy of them. "These rights must be defined in their respective contexts. For example, the keys of the ministering of angels are available to all Aaronic Priesthood holders by right (see D&C 13:1),"[15] and all worthy members of the Church may receive the blessings of this right or responsibility. In other words, the Aaronic Priesthood holder has the responsibility by right to turn the key of the ministering of angels, making it possible for all worthy, covenant-keeping members to have the ministering of angels. These keys are distinct from keys of presidency, as all Aaronic Priesthood holders have this key, regardless of whether or not they are the president of a quorum. The key of the ministering of angels, therefore, is not a key of presidency, as those who hold this key do not preside by virtue of receiving it. As President Oaks inquired, "How does the Aaronic Priesthood hold the key to the ministering of angels?" He then answered his own question:

> Through the Aaronic Priesthood ordinances of baptism and the sacrament, we are cleansed of our sins and promised that if we keep our covenants we will always have His Spirit to be with us. I believe that promise not only refers to the Holy Ghost but also to the ministering of angels, for "angels speak by the power of the Holy Ghost; wherefore, they speak the words of Christ" (2 Ne. 32:3). So it is that those who hold the Aaronic Priesthood open the door for all Church members who worthily partake of the sacrament to enjoy the companionship of the Spirit of the Lord and the ministering of angels.[16]

President M. Russell Ballard further taught: "All who have made sacred covenants with the Lord and who honor those covenants are eligible to receive personal revelation, to be blessed by the ministering of angels, to commune with God, to receive the fulness of the gospel, and, ultimately, to become heirs alongside Jesus Christ of all our Father has."[17] These privileges stated by President Ballard are usually taught in context of those who hold the priesthood or who have priesthood keys, such as those holding the Aaronic Priesthood, or elders serving as missionaries. Again, these keys are not the keys of presidency, but rather, general priesthood keys given to ordained Aaronic Priesthood holders.

I have read and listened to many talks in which the young men

> *It is critical to not only teach the young men about what it means to hold the keys of the ministering of angels, but to also teach both the young women and young men what it means to have the ministering of angels in their lives.*

have been told how significant it is that they have the right to the ministering of angels. Although this is correct, so do the young women! All may receive the ministering of angels based upon their ability to make and keep sacred covenants associated with baptism and every other covenant. What an incredible privilege our eight-year-old Primary girls could and should understand. It is critical to not only teach the young men about what it means to hold the keys of the ministering of angels, but to also teach both the young women and young men what it means to have the ministering of angels in their lives. Imagine the blessings a young woman could have as she is going through the early stages of maturation to know that she has the privilege of having angels, seen or unseen, accompany her, know her, and speak to her. In a recent class I taught, I asked fifty students, thirty-five of whom were female, "Who has the privilege of the ministering of angels?" Not one female student in the class raised her hand. How different the lives of these thirty-five young adult, mostly returned sister missionaries and young mothers could have been over the last decade of their lives, had they better understood this truth.

The following table is my attempt to put these keys in better context and clarify what we can.

## APOSTOLIC KEYS

**When were these keys received?**
Peter, James, and John restored the keys of the Melchizedek Priesthood in 1829, bestowing apostolic authority and keys (see D&C 18:9; 27:12–13). In 1836 Moses, Elias, and Elijah restored additional keys.

**Who holds these keys?**
Prophet, First Presidency, members of the Quorum of the Twelve, and any man ordained to the office of Apostle.

**Over whom do these key holders preside?**
Everyone in the world.

**Who receives the blessings of these keys?**
All people in the world who obey the teachings of the prophets and apostles.

### KEYS OF PRESIDENCY

**When were these keys received?**
Restoration of Aaronic and Melchizedek Priesthoods.

**Who holds these keys?**
Presidents of temples, missions, stakes, and districts; bishops; branch presidents; and quorum presidents.

**Over whom do these key holders preside?**
Those over whom they've been called to preside, generally limited by specific calling, geography, and time.

**Who receives the blessings of these keys?**
All within the bounds of the key holder's responsibility.

### GENERAL PRIESTHOOD HOLDER KEYS

**When were these keys received?**
Restoration of Aaronic and Melchizedek Priesthoods.

**Who holds these keys?**
Those ordained to an office in the priesthood.

**Over whom do these key holders preside?**
Since these keys are not "presiding keys," they are not associated with stewardship. Rather, all who partake of ordinances associated with these keys are blessed by them.

**Who receives the blessings of these keys?**
All who make and keep covenants associated with the ordinances.

Let us now go back to the question of "who in this classroom holds priesthood keys?" There is simply not a cut-and-dried answer to this question; it varies depending on what priesthood keys we are referring to. Frankly, I'm confident that at the time I asked the question, neither my students nor I knew the answer. Due to the age of these students, had I asked, "Who in this class holds the priesthood keys of presidency?" most likely only those students who were either bishops or elders quorum presidents would have raised their hands. Typically there are few, if any, in a group of young adults who hold these specific priesthood keys of presidency.

In addition to the priesthood keys listed above, it is also important to note that there are nearly forty different uses of the term *key* in the scriptures, not all of which are referring to priesthood keys. Many of these keys could better be described as rights, privileges, or blessings of the priesthood that are available to all worthy members (or, in the case of the temple, worthy endowed members). These keys do not require priesthood ordination but rather "are provided to the seeker of truth and righteousness" through the priesthood. "Each of these keys must be qualified for and sought after for them to be manifest in the life of the individual."[18] These keys or rights will be discussed later.

Finally, there are other keys listed in the scriptures that are less known. They have varied purposes and significance, but it is still important to recognize their existence. They include, for example, "the key of the bottomless pit" (Revelation 20:1), "grand keys" or key words (Doctrine and Covenants 129:9; 130:11), "keys of the treasury" (1 Nephi 4:20).

Perhaps one of the most important truths regarding priesthood keys is the purpose for which priesthood keys are delegated. In a worldwide training broadcast on the priesthood, Elder Donald L. Hallstrom of the Presidency of the Seventy instructed: "Our greatest responsibility as leaders who hold keys is to help fathers in the home, mothers in the home, youth. And we're really supplemental to the very important work that goes on in the home."[19]

## PRESIDING PRIESTHOOD KEYS AND AUTHORITY ARE DELEGATED IN A TRANSPARENT ORDER

One of the compliments I hear from members and leaders of other faiths regarding The Church of Jesus Christ of Latter-day Saints pertains to how organized and structured we are. There is a clear head, an organized body of leaders, and a general recognition of who these leaders are. Many have expressed how they have been blessed by a ward member who contacts a direct leader, such as a Relief Society president or elders quorum president (although they don't use these titles), who then contacts a bishop or stake president, and before they know it, problems are solved. On many occasions, as I have spoken with leaders and friends of other faiths, they have complimented the Church on its organizational structure and associated effectiveness, especially in caring for the one.

As members of the Church, we are fairly familiar with the general structure of the Church. We understand its hierarchical nature. For the most part, if we have callings or assignments, we know to whom we should report and whom we are to serve. In Christ's Church, there is order in all things. Christ made this clear through two experiences from Church history that are recorded in the Doctrine and Covenants, in sections 28 and 43, respectively. During this time in Church history (1830–31), the organizational structure had not clearly been revealed. It is in large part because of these two experiences that we understand the organizational structure of the Church, including who is at the head, and even the structure of the delegation of priesthood keys of presidency and priesthood authority.

Hiram Page was an early member of the Church and one of the Eight Witnesses of the Book of Mormon. He believed he had a stone that gave him revelation for the Church, and many became confused and followed him. The Lord gave a revelation through Joseph Smith for Oliver Cowdery, Page's brother-in-law, to talk with him and help him see that it was only Joseph Smith who had the authority to receive commandments and revelation for the entire Church. In this revelation, the Lord also made it clear that Joseph was "the head of the Church" and was to preside, "for all things must be done in order," the Lord declared (Doctrine and Covenants 28:6, 13). Hiram was humble and repentant, and he came back to the Church. This revelation clarified for the first time that God intended for Joseph, or the prophet, to be the one leading and guiding the Church.

A few months later, a Mrs. Hubble, like Hiram Page, believed she had authority to speak for the Lord. As with Hiram, many believed her. The Prophet again inquired of the Lord as to what to do regarding this situation. In response, the Lord told the members of the Church through Joseph that he, the Prophet, was appointed to receive revelation for the Church, and that the members should not be deceived. The Lord declared, "He that is ordained of me shall come in at the gate and be ordained as I have told you before, to teach those revelations which you have received and shall receive through him whom I have appointed" (Doctrine and

Covenants 43:2–7). This revelation, according to President Dallin H. Oaks, excluded the "possibility of secret callings or appointments to receive revelation."[20] In other words, "coming in at the gate" meant that there was no hiding or secrecy regarding leadership and revelation. Therefore, as members of the Church, we do not need to be confused as to who presides, who has authority, and what that authority is for. Although Mrs. Hubble had "made a deep impression on the minds of many"—so much so that it was said that a "barbed arrow which she left in the hearts of some, [was] not as yet eradicated"[21]—this need not be the case with us.

President Marion G. Romney gave these four simple principles to keep in mind when determining if a revelation is from God: First, "Does it purport to originate in the wisdom of men, or was it revealed from heaven?" Second, "Does the teaching bear the proper label?" Third, "The teaching must not only come under the proper label, but it must also conform to the other teaching of the Gospel of Jesus Christ." Fourth, "Does it come through the proper Church channel?"[22] The final simple test is absolutely critical in our day. With so much information coming over the Internet, so many voices purposefully, innocently, or naively declaring falsehoods as truth, so much ethical relativism, we must know the correct source of information. There is no question in my mind that Christ organized His Church in this day, with apostles and prophets as the head and a clear and transparent organizational structure, knowing the calamities and confusion that would be imminent.

A few years ago a couple of students came to me and told me there was a gentleman who wanted to speak with me after class. They said they believed he had an inside scoop on some of the teachings of the Church that could be beneficial to me. When I returned to my office after class, I found the man standing outside my door. When I reached the door, and was thus in close proximity to him, he whispered, "I know of some things that I have never shared with anyone, but that are critical for you to know as a religion professor."

Although I knew the answer before I asked, I inquired, "Are the Brethren aware of these teachings?"

"No," came his quick and defensive response, "they are not yet ready to receive it." Although the man continued to explain to me the "truths" he was individually given, his teachings landed on deaf ears. Not only did the spirit of discernment clearly teach me that this man was deceptive and his teachings were not of God, but the administrative order of the Church, as taught in the scriptures and by living prophets, made it clear that this man's teachings were not in accordance with the will of God. This man did not hold the keys of the holy apostleship, and therefore he did not have authority to declare doctrine for the Church.

For various reasons, there have always been those who have gone beyond their stewardship in regard to authority in the Church. Some of these are intentional deceptions; others are a result of mental illness or of people thinking they have powers beyond the abilities of others. During my life I have known many members who have been confused about this basic principle. Some have truly believed others' claims of special gifts of revelation or leadership, and have followed those individuals instead of the teachings of Church leaders. But regardless of how persuasive, intelligent, or kind people may be, the Lord has an order He follows. Following someone outside of this order is dangerous and against the plan of God.

The following chart clarifies in a precise manner the conferral of priesthood keys and authority. Note that the Presidency of the Seventy are delegated priesthood keys allowing them to preside over the Quorums of the Seventy, but these keys are not used to preside over stake presidents and bishops. Those keys used to preside over the stake presidents and bishops are delegated keys used to act in behalf of the Quorum of the Twelve on a specific assignment. Only the bishop has presiding keys over the ward. The Young Men's president, Young Women's president, Relief Society president, Sunday School president, Primary president, and ward mission leader are all delegated priesthood authority. Although the elders quorum president is delegated priesthood keys of presidency through the stake president, he does not preside and has no authority over members of the ward outside of his quorum. It is also interesting to note that although mission presidents hold priesthood keys of presidency over the missionaries within the mission, some additional keys are delegated to them based on assignment by the First Presidency and Quorum of the Twelve Apostles.

# CONFERRAL OF PRIESTHOOD KEYS and CONFERRAL OF AUTHORITY

## PRIESTHOOD POWER IN THE CHURCH

Prior to His entrance into mortality, Christ declared that He was coming "to do the will, both of the Father and of the Son" (3 Nephi 1:14). The last words Christ uttered in mortality, "Father, it is finished, thy will is done" (JST, Matthew 27:50), were echoed as He told the Nephites after His Crucifixion, "I have suffered the will of the Father in all things from the beginning" (3 Nephi 11:11). It was in submitting His will and power to the Father's that He gained His greatest power. Indeed, the many miracles Christ performed in mortality were swallowed up in one of the most significant decisions the Savior ever made: when He turned His will over to the Father in His most critical hour, thus making the salvation of all mankind possible. In that moment, He also made it possible for us, as Heavenly Father's children, to increase in power as we follow Christ's example.

"The closer we are to Jesus Christ in the thoughts and intents of our hearts," Elder Dale G. Renlund instructed, "the more we appreciate His innocent suffering, the more grateful we are for grace and forgiveness, and the more we want to repent and become like Him."[23] I would add that the more we strive to become like Him, the more power we receive.

President Russell M. Nelson communicated the stretching necessary to receive God's power: "When the Savior knows that you truly want to reach up to Him, when He can feel that the greatest desire of your heart is to draw His power into your life, you will be led by the Holy Ghost to know exactly what you should do."[24] The Savior Himself understands what it means to stretch. Elder Neal A. Maxwell taught, "Jesus' brief stumbling while carrying the cross is a reminder as to how close to the very edge of our strength God stretches us at times."[25] This desire to receive God's power, coupled with our faith in Jesus Christ, propels us to do things we otherwise would not do. For, according to President Nelson, "Faith that motivates us to action gives us more access to His power."[26] Therefore, as we strive to become like Christ, stretching, acting in faith, learning, and obeying, we are more likely to gain priesthood power. Sister Julie B. Beck, former General Relief Society President, reminded us that "priesthood is God's power" and therefore is available to all members, both male and female, who "make and keep covenants."[27]

There is a price to be paid to develop priesthood power. President Nelson instructed that the more we develop Christlike attributes such as "faith, virtue, knowledge, temperance, patience, godliness, brotherly kindness, charity, [obedience,] and diligence," then "the greater will be our priesthood power." President Nelson also taught other ways to increase our power in the priesthood. These include praying "from our hearts," even praying "*to know how to pray* for more power," promising that those who so ask will be taught by the Lord. Searching the scriptures and feasting upon the words of Christ, worshipping regularly in the temple, and serving others also increase priesthood power, according to President Nelson. "If we will humbly present ourselves before the Lord and ask Him to teach us, He will show us how to increase *our* access to *His* power."[28]

Some of the most poignant lessons Joseph Smith learned were taught to him by the Lord in Liberty Jail, or, as some refer to it, the temple prison. One of these many teachings engraved on Joseph's heart had reference to priesthood power:

> The rights of the priesthood are inseparably connected with the powers of heaven, and . . . the *powers* of heaven cannot be controlled nor handled only upon the principles of righteousness. . . . When we undertake to cover our sins, or to gratify our pride, our vain ambition, or to exercise control or dominion or compulsion upon the souls of the children of men, in any degree of unrighteousness, behold, the heavens withdraw themselves; the Spirit of the Lord is grieved; and when it is withdrawn, Amen to the priesthood or the authority of that man. (Doctrine and Covenants 121:36–37; emphasis added)

Regardless of ordination to priesthood office, or priesthood authority received through being set apart or receiving temple ordinances, righteousness is a prerequisite to priesthood power. In fact, as the Prophet Joseph was preparing women to enter the temple, he reminded them of the importance of righteousness in regard to the temple and priesthood they would receive, expressing sentiments similar to those in Doctrine and Covenants 121, such as: "We are full of selfishness—the devil flatters us that we are very righteous, while we are feeding on the faults of others," and "By union of feeling we obtain pow'r with God."[29] For both women and men, priesthood power is gained through righteousness and lost through unrighteousness.

## CONCLUSION

Our Father in Heaven is a God of order. Jesus Christ is the holder of all priesthood authority, keys, and power. The purpose of God's priesthood is for the salvation of individuals and exaltation of families. In order to have full access to God's authority, power, and blessings, we, as members of the Church, must live according to His commandments. These are His laws, unchanged by man, and used to bless the entire human race.

Chapter 3

# "WHAT OTHER AUTHORITY CAN IT BE?"
## Connecting Women with Priesthood at Church

Before going through how different parts of the priesthood apply to women at Church, let's look at some realistic and pertinent questions people have asked, and then answer them using the principles and doctrines just discussed.

- Should young women as well as young men be able to bless and pass the sacrament?
- Do a sister missionary and an elder both have the same authority granted to them to teach the gospel to investigators?
- If a stake Young Men president and a stake Young Women president are in a meeting, does the Young Men president preside due to his ordination to a priesthood office?
- If a husband and a wife are called to teach a Sunday School class together, does the husband preside, based on what the family proclamation teaches?
- Is it incorrect to thank the "priesthood" (referring to the brethren) for passing the sacrament after the young men have participated in this sacred ordinance?
- Is it appropriate for a Relief Society president from one ward

to give instruction to a Relief Society president of another ward regarding her calling?
- Was the oath and covenant of the priesthood meant only for men?
- Are keys of presidency held by men only?
- If a deacons quorum president and a Beehive class president are in a planning meeting, with no other supervision, who presides?
- If a Relief Society president and an elders quorum president are working on ministering assignments for the ward, and the elders quorum president feels he should create a companionship out of a husband and wife, can he do so because of the keys and responsibilities he has, without consulting the Relief Society president?
- Is it appropriate for a woman who has been counseling with a bishop to continue to counsel with that bishop after he has been released?
- Since the relationship between husband and wife is critical, when a husband or wife receives a calling, should it be understood and expected that confidential matters will be discussed between the two of them?
- Although only men hold priesthood keys and are ordained to priesthood offices, are women essential for the salvation of God's children in the Church, outside of the bearing and nurturing of children?
- Although only men are given keys of presidency, are there others called of God who receive revelation for others, such as women with spiritual gifts?

# PRIESTHOOD AUTHORITY AND WOMEN AT CHURCH

Both women and men are blessed by those who have priesthood authority.

# "WHAT OTHER AUTHORITY CAN IT BE?"

## Priesthood Authority through Ordination Blesses All

Without priesthood holders, we would be unable to participate in any of the ordinances of the Church, including baptism, confirmation and bestowal of the gift of the Holy Ghost, sacrament, initiatory ordinances, endowments, and sealings. Frankly, there would be no Church and no members of the Church if men were not authorized to use the priesthood to perform certain functions. There would be no remission of sins, no priesthood blessings, no gifts of the Spirit, no full-time missionaries, no prophet to lead the Church. All of us have been blessed tremendously by those who have been ordained to priesthood offices. Without them, there would be no Primary, no Young Women program, no Relief Society, and, most important, families could not be eternal. How grateful I am for those in my life who have worthily used the priesthood authority they have received through being ordained to priesthood offices within the Church!

> Without priesthood holders, we would be unable to participate in any of the ordinances of the Church, including baptism, confirmation and bestowal of the gift of the Holy Ghost, sacrament, initiatory ordinances, endowments, and sealings. Frankly, there would be no Church and no members of the Church if men were not authorized to use the priesthood to perform certain functions.

## Women Receive Priesthood Authority by Being Set Apart

As a young sister missionary, having been set apart by my father, who was the stake president, I wondered how it was that I was able to preach the gospel to the wonderful people of Los Angeles when I did not have the authority of the priesthood as the ordained elders did. I obediently taught the gospel and felt the influence of the Spirit strongly, even to exhorting and promising, but I wondered how that was possible, if I had no priesthood authority to do so. I understood that I was not ordained to a priesthood office and therefore could not perform priesthood ordinances outside the temple, but still I felt I had authority—being a full-time, set-apart, assigned-by-the-prophet missionary—to help people obtain salvation. I even felt, although I didn't understand how, that I was authorized by the Lord to do so.

On many occasions, when I read in Alma 17 how Alma and the sons of Mosiah met after fourteen years of preaching the gospel, I remember thinking that I too would like to bring "many to the knowledge of the truth," and I hoped to also be an instrument in God's hands and to help others be "brought before the altar of God, to call on his name and confess their sins before him" (v. 4), as did the sons of Mosiah. Like the sons of Mosiah, I too "had searched the scriptures diligently, that [I] might know the word of God" (v. 2), and "had given [myself] to much prayer, and fasting," and even felt that I too "had the spirit of prophecy, and the spirit of revelation." But I was confused, knowing that I was not an ordained priesthood holder and therefore assuming (incorrectly) that I did not teach "with power and authority of God" (v. 3). Like Nephi, "I pray[ed] continually for [my investigators] by day, and mine eyes water[ed] my pillow by night, because of them; and I [cried] unto my God in faith, and I [knew] that he [would] hear my cry" (2 Nephi 33:3). Yet I often wondered how I could be an effective missionary like Nephi if I wasn't ordained to a priesthood office.

On one occasion, I sat next to my companion, a wise, experienced, humble, worthy, intelligent, truth-seeking, and bold sister, when she warned an investigator that "if he did not obey the promptings of the Holy Ghost at that moment, God would hold him accountable in the next life." Although this may not always be the case, in this moment, both the investigator and I knew and felt that she spoke with God's authority. He was baptized, and we were all grateful.

It wasn't until years later, when I heard President Dallin H. Oaks speak regarding authority of the priesthood, that I realized what I felt was actually correct. My companion and I and all sister missionaries had priesthood authority because we had been called and set apart by a stake president who held priesthood keys of presidency, and we were working under the direction of the mission president, who also held priesthood keys of presidency for missionaries. Although we were not ordained to the office of elder, which authorizes a Melchizedek Priesthood holder to baptize and confirm, we were set apart as full-time missionaries, which gave us the authority of God to teach and bring people to Christ.

## Men and Women Have Equal Priesthood Authority in Their Callings Unless Otherwise Delegated by the One Holding the Priesthood Key of Presidency

When teaching this concept to my students, I often ask, "If a stake is having a combined Young Men and Young Women presidency meeting at which no member of the stake presidency is present, and no one has specifically been appointed to preside in the meeting, who presides?" Because both the stake Young Women president and the stake Young Men president were called and set apart by one holding priesthood keys of presidency (the stake president or one of his counselors who has delegated responsibility to do so), both the Young Men president and the Young Women president have equal priesthood authority for their respective callings. Since neither of them holds keys of presidency, unless otherwise specified by the priesthood key holder, neither presides over the other. Presiding then becomes a decision made by the two of them working together.

I remember vividly my first trek meeting after being called as the stake Young Women president. The stake Young Men president asked if his stake Young Men presidency and my Young Women presidency could meet to start getting on the same page regarding the youth trek that was to be held the next summer. After introducing ourselves, the Young Men president simply stated, "Sister Morgan, as you are new to this calling, may I suggest that I preside at this meeting? At the next meeting, we would appreciate it if you would be willing to preside." I admit that it caught me by surprise that a stake Young Men leader, who was recently released as a mission president, who had previously served as a bishop and stake president, and who clearly had much more Church leadership experience than I did as a single sister in my early thirties, would invite me to preside at our next meeting.

Frankly, I believe it was *because* of his Church leadership positions and his mature understanding of priesthood keys of presidency and priesthood authority that he did make the suggestion. I'm grateful for his wisdom and humility, and I'm confident that his understanding and character helped all of us work as a team and focus our attention on being instruments in the hands of the Lord to save the souls of the youth in that stake.

## Presiding in Church Callings Is Not Determined by Gender

Presiding in the Church isn't dependent upon the male gender or even ordination, but is a matter of the functioning of priesthood keys of presidency. If a husband and a wife, for example, were called to be team teachers to the same Primary class, neither the husband nor the wife would preside over the other in the class. It has often been misunderstood that the phrase *the priesthood presides* refers to men possessing authority over women. The priesthood is not a man, and since both the man and the woman in this case have priesthood authority through one who holds priesthood keys of presidency, they both preside in the class. It would be completely appropriate for either the husband or the wife to call on someone in the class to pray, and it would be appropriate for each of them to take turns teaching the lesson without either of them dictating who will do what.

## Men Are No More "The Priesthood" Than Women Are

As Elder Neil L. Andersen taught: "A man may open the drapes, so the warm sunlight comes into the room, but the man does not own the sun or the light or the warmth it brings. The blessings of the priesthood are infinitely greater than the one who is asked to administer the gift."[1] Recently, in a sacrament meeting I attended, following the passing of the sacrament, the bishopric member thanked the "the young men for passing the sacrament." I almost shouted for joy, as it was one of the first times I had heard a member of the bishopric not thank "the priesthood for passing the sacrament." As President Oaks and other leaders have repeated over and over, "Men are not the priesthood."[2]

Men may have been ordained to an office of the priesthood—they may have had the priesthood conferred upon them—but they are not the priesthood any more than the women are the priesthood. Priesthood is not something we are. It is God's power that He authorizes His servants to use for the benefit of others. It would be just as incorrect, after a group of young women performed a musical number, to thank the priesthood (referring to the sisters) for singing as it is for someone to thank the priesthood (referring to the men) for passing the sacrament. The priesthood didn't sing, and the priesthood didn't pass the sacrament. People did!

Although this admonition of not calling men "the priesthood" has been repeated over and over in general settings, members still struggle to get out of this incorrect habit. In May of 2016 I was asked to speak at the BYU Women's Conference on the topic of "Blessings of the Priesthood for All." As I was walking up to campus, an active, well-meaning gentleman in my ward asked me if I was going to mention the truth that men are not the priesthood, to which I responded in the affirmative. He replied, "I don't understand why calling men the priesthood is such a big deal. It's simply tradition and does no harm. It seems that we are making such a big deal out of something so insignificant." A short discussion between the two of us ensued on the sidewalk. We discussed the definition of the priesthood and how no human being is perfect. We then talked of the dangers that could arise and have arisen, and the negative implications that have occurred, when unworthy, abusive, hypocritical, or even worthy but imperfect men become leaders and especially fathers. We agreed that we both knew many people—especially women, youth, and children—who struggled with the idea of fathers and leaders using the priesthood as an excuse for or even a weapon of immoral behavior. We concluded that even if a man was perfect, calling any mortal "the priesthood" is demeaning to the power of God.

## Priesthood Authority Is Limited by Jurisdiction for Men and Women

When I was serving as a stake Young Women president, I remember often hearing of what other stake Young Women presidents were doing with their young women. Although I appreciated the help from other

Young Women leaders from other stakes, I recognized that I had priesthood authority for my stake young women under the stake president's priesthood keys of presidency, and I needed to be receiving revelation for my young women. This would be the case for all auxiliary leaders and members in various callings.

Priesthood authority is also limited by time. Shortly after being called to be the stake Young Women president, I went to the past stake Young Women president and asked her opinion and advice. Although she was able to provide lots of information, which was the basis for much of the inspiration I would need in the future, she was unable, as she had been released, to receive revelation for the young women. I found it fascinating that during the time I was the president of the Young Women, the Lord blessed me to be able to remember the names of the young women like I never had before and has even blessed me to remember many of them since.

## Both Men and Women Alike Receive All of the Blessings of the Priesthood

Quoting President Joseph Fielding Smith, President M. Russell Ballard carefully instructed: "The blessings of the priesthood are not confined to men alone. These blessings are also poured out upon . . . all the faithful women of the Church. . . . The Lord offers to his daughters *every* spiritual gift and blessing that can be obtained by his sons."[3] Thus, any time a priesthood holder is promised blessings associated with holding the priesthood, these blessings can be applied to every covenant-keeping member, including women not ordained to priesthood offices. It is important for all Church members to know that, regardless of priesthood ordination, they can be blessed to receive "all that my Father hath." For those teaching the gospel, regardless of gender,

> It is important for all Church members to know that, regardless of priesthood ordination, they can be blessed to receive "all that my Father hath."

God promises that He "will go before your face." He also promises, "I will be on your right hand and on your left, and my Spirit shall be in your hearts, and mine angels round about you, to bear you up" (Doctrine and Covenants 84:38, 88).

In the Church, therefore, it is equally important for both girls and boys to understand priesthood, priesthood authority, priesthood keys, and priesthood power. It is important not only to encourage the boys to prepare to be ordained to an office in the priesthood, but also to teach both young men and young women to be righteous in order to use the priesthood authority granted to them and to have priesthood power in their callings, perhaps while they are still in Primary.

## PRIESTHOOD KEYS OF PRESIDENCY AND WOMEN AT CHURCH

President Oaks instructed that "all priesthood authority *in the Church* functions under the direction of the one who holds the appropriate priesthood keys."[4]

### Priesthood Keys of Presidency Give the Key Holder the Authority to Preside over Those for Whom He Has Stewardship

The experience associated with my mission call and first assignment as a missionary has been a poignant lesson to me regarding this principle. From as early as I could remember, my desire always was to serve a full-time mission for the Church. When I was a young BYU student, the desire became even stronger, especially as I watched my male friends receive their mission calls. During one semester, however, I had a very difficult roommate experience. Up to this point, I had felt that, although I wasn't perfect, I basically got along with most people. It never occurred to me that having a companion could be a difficult thing. During my mission interview with my stake president, who was my father, he asked me where I wanted to serve. Just months before, one of these roommates that we lived with had received a mission call to the California Los Angeles Mission. She was assigned to serve at the visitors' center, and to proselytize and teach the gospel in Spanish. Although we were still good friends, the roommate situation was difficult, and I wanted to stay as far away from those memories as possible. In response to my father's question, as a well-taught young adult, I simply responded that I would go anywhere the Lord wanted me to go. Perhaps against protocol, my stake president then asked, "Where do you *not* want to go?" Without a moment of hesitation, I blurted out, "The only place I do not want to be assigned is to the Los Angeles California Temple visitors' center, speaking Spanish."

To this day, my father still assures me that he did not write anything of the sort on my papers. In fact, he said he selfishly suggested that I be sent to Wales, as that would allow me to be among our ancestors. My six older siblings who served missions before me were all called on foreign missions. I put on my paper that I desired to serve "foreign" as well. A few weeks later, I was speaking at a stake youth fireside and my parents handed me the envelope in front of all of the youth and leaders. I opened it immediately, but anxiously, as I knew by the weight that my call likely wasn't foreign. Having read many mission calls, I knew exactly where to turn my attention. Before even having a chance to read the letter out loud, I began to cry. Everyone in the audience thought I was shedding tears of joy, but my parents knew otherwise. Standing close beside me, my dad wisely asked if I was okay. I whispered, "I just received my worst nightmare!"

"Los Angeles?" he asked. As I nodded, he continued, "Visitors' center?" Tears continued to stream down my cheeks. "Spanish speaking?" I could tell he was just as shocked as I was distraught! I nodded my head again, and he looked at me somewhat bewildered. I gained my composure and read the letter out loud. Following lots of pats and hugs by youth and leaders, I found a quiet place and began to read my patriarchal blessing. The Spirit confirmed to me that although I did not understand the reason for this call, the call was assigned by an Apostle who held apostolic keys, and this was the Lord's will for me.

A couple of months later, my father, still serving as the stake president, became extremely ill and would be unable to set me apart as a full-time missionary. With other personal circumstances, including my sister being diagnosed with stage 4 breast cancer and the diagnosis giving her only six months to live, I began to question my choice to serve a mission. With my dad being ill and unable to set me apart or even give me a

## "WHAT OTHER AUTHORITY CAN IT BE?"

father's blessing, I reached out to my bishop. We discussed my decision briefly. Then, turning the key in my behalf, he told me he felt that the Lord desired that I not postpone my mission. He then gave me a blessing, which stated, among other things, that while I was away serving the Lord, He would bless my family, and I would return to see them whole. That He would perform miracles in my family's behalf as a result of my service. That the timing of my calling was critical for the companions I would have and the people we would teach.

Later that evening, the bishop returned to give my father a blessing. He blessed my father, among other things, that he would be healed long enough to set me apart as a full-time missionary. That evening, my father, serving as my stake president, who held priesthood keys of presidency, stood healthy and strong behind me, with my bishop as his companion, and set me apart as a full-time missionary. The next morning, my parents dropped me off at the airport.

After spending six weeks at the Provo Missionary Training Center, I was off to the California Los Angeles Mission. Greeted by the mission president and his wife, all of the new missionaries and all of our future trainers met together in one of the large rooms of the visitors' center. I'll never forget how our mission president explained to us that never before had he received such clear inspiration regarding companionships. He then started calling off new missionaries and their trainers. My name was announced, and the name of my old roommate was announced as my trainer. We met each other in the room, hugged, and for the next while, as we drove to our new area, made amends for any negative experiences or feelings we had previously had. The Lord, through an Apostle, stake president, bishop, and mission president, who all held priesthood keys of presidency, resolved the only relationship trouble I had ever had to that point. The first two doors we knocked on were opened to us. Two weeks later, both individuals who had greeted us at the door were baptized. One year later, almost to the date, both of these individuals and their families entered the Los Angeles California Temple, received their endowments, and were sealed to their families. My old roommate, companion, dear friend, and I were there to witness the experience.

About six months later I returned home to find my sister, although bald, still alive and thriving with her new baby and husband, and my father, although now released as a stake president and retired from his profession, healthy and strong. The man who had been my bishop when I left was now my stake president. With the keys he then held, he released me from full-time missionary service. I returned to BYU to become roommates once again with my past roommate, companion, mentor, and dear friend. All of this was made possible through the priesthood keys of presidency used in behalf of those for whom the key holders had stewardship.

## Priesthood Keys of Presidency Are Limited by Geography or Boundaries

President Oaks instructed, "Church organizations like wards, quorums, or auxiliaries always have geographic boundaries that limit the responsibility and authority of the callings associated with them."[5] The prophet or President of the Church, for example, holds keys that allow him to preside for the entire world while he is mortal. His geographic boundaries are the earth, including those who previously lived on the earth and have now passed beyond the veil. President Nelson demonstrated this in the April 2018 general conference, when he spoke to those on both sides of the veil.[6] Although Apostles hold all the same keys as the prophet does, they are authorized to use them only as assigned by the prophet. Mission presidents hold keys for all of the missionaries in the mission and those people preparing for baptism; bishops hold keys for everyone in the ward boundaries; and quorum presidents hold keys for those in their quorums.

The stake president in a stake presides in that stake because he is the key holder for that stake. If that same stake president were to go to another stake in which that stake's Relief Society president was holding a meeting, she, although she does not have keys, would still be in charge or presiding in that meeting. He has keys over his stake, but not hers. It would not be appropriate for him to sit on the stand or call on someone to pray, as it is not in his geographic boundary. The fact that he is a man, even a man holding keys, does not make him the presiding authority outside of his own jurisdiction.

Since the combining of elders and high priests into one quorum—the elders quorum—I have heard a few women share confusing experiences. One Relief Society president shared with me that she had prayed about a ministering assignment for one of the sisters in her ward, and, after giving her the assignment, was told by the sister that she had already been assigned by the elders quorum president to teach another family with her husband and didn't feel she could do both. Although the intentions and motivation of the elders quorum president were likely admirable, he had overstepped his bounds. Unlike the bishop, whose keys are over the entire ward, the elders quorum president's keys are over his quorum. Therefore, unless he had consulted with the Relief Society president and both of them had agreed, he should not have asked a member of the Relief Society to accept a ministering assignment. That assignment falls under the responsibility of the Relief Society president.

Recently, when discussing the keys of the priesthood with my students, I asked, "If a deacons quorum president and a Beehive class president are planning a youth activity together, and there is no other person in the room, who presides in that meeting?" Without hesitation, the majority of the students confidently answered, "The deacons quorum president."

"Why?" I asked.

Their quick response: "Because he holds keys."

"Whom does he hold keys over?" came my reply.

Then the pause. Quickly the students understood that, unlike the bishop, who holds keys over the entire ward, the deacons quorum president holds keys only over his quorum; therefore, he has no authority over the Beehive class president. Neither is in charge of the other. In fact, the Beehive class president has stewardship over her class, and the deacons quorum president has stewardship over his quorum. It is important to teach the deacons quorum president his duties and responsibilities as one who holds keys, but it is equally important to teach the Beehive class president her duties and responsibilities as she has been called and set apart and given priesthood authority to preside over the Beehives in her class.

## Priesthood Keys of Presidency Are Limited by Time

There is an axiom or phrase in the Church that, although true, is commonly misunderstood: "Once a bishop, always a bishop." The truth is that because "bishop" is an ordained Melchizedek Priesthood office conferred by the laying on of hands, he will always hold that office, similar to that of an elder or high priest.

The confusion comes, however, when a bishop is released from his calling as a bishop and returns to the elders quorum, and a new bishop is called. Although it may be technically still appropriate to *call* the man bishop, as he has been ordained to that office, it would not be appropriate for him to *act* as bishop, as he no longer holds the priesthood keys of presidency or authority of that calling.

I remember talking with one of my dear friends following his release as bishop. I asked him what lessons he had learned through that calling. He mentioned that one of the lessons was the reality of priesthood keys and the mantle of a bishop. "When I was called," he explained, "I felt the authority of the keys. I was blessed with the gift of discernment, was a judge in Israel, and was blessed with the authority of the bishop. The moment I was released," he shared, "those gifts and that feeling of the reality of authority through those priesthood keys immediately vanished. I clearly am no longer the bishop of the ward."

> It is important to teach the deacons quorum president his duties and responsibilities as one who holds keys, but it is equally important to teach the Beehive class president her duties and responsibilities as she has been called and set apart and given priesthood authority to preside over the Beehives in her class.

## Timings of Calls and Releases Are Determined by One Holding Keys of Presidency

President Oaks taught: "In the Church, a priesthood leader who holds the necessary keys has the authority to call or release persons serving under his direction. He can even cause that they lose their membership and have their names 'blotted out' (see Mosiah 26:34–38; Alma 5:56–62)."[7] Whether it relates to a nursery leader, a Relief Society teacher, a general auxiliary leader, or a member of the First Presidency, the initiation and termination of a calling are determined by the key holder, not the individual. (There may be circumstances, of which the bishop is ignorant, when the individual would be unable to function in that assignment. The individual certainly has the right to discuss such concerns with the bishop.) Once a person has been released from a calling, he or she no longer holds the keys or authority for that calling and therefore no longer has the responsibility or stewardship of that calling.

## Priesthood Keys of Presidency Do Not Apply to a Person's Spouse

President Oaks taught that one of the most significant differences between priesthood authority at home and at Church is that of partnership.[8] I recently asked a class of students how partnership works with the priesthood at Church and in the home. To my surprise, one of my female students related that her husband served in a young married student ward bishopric. As his wife, she explained, she also had stewardship over the ward. Neither she nor her husband held priesthood keys, but since they were married, they shared in the responsibility. She explained that although her husband went to the meetings and conducted interviews and so on, they still acted as a team with equal authority.

Carefully, I complimented her on her desire to serve the ward and be such an important member, and also complimented her on understanding of what partnership in the home could look like. But I was then quick to help her and the rest of the class understand that partnership in priesthood authority at Church is not the same as partnership in priesthood authority at home. Although men and women must work together to effectively oversee the programs of the Church both generally and locally, each member of the Church has a specific calling for which he or she is given priesthood authority. A wife would have no more stewardship over her husband's bishopric calling than he would have over hers if she were the ward Relief Society president and he were a Sunday School teacher.

They may counsel with each other and learn from each other, but the authority for each calling belongs to the individual.

In relating instances in which priesthood authority is confused, President Oaks related: "I have also seen some faithful women who misunderstand how priesthood authority functions. Mindful of their partnership relationship with their husband in the family, some wives have sought to extend that relationship to their husband's priesthood calling, such as bishop or mission president." He explains that, although this partnership relationship does exist in the family, it does not exist in the Church.[9] When a man is extended a calling where priesthood keys are involved, the associated authority is his and not his wife's.

The role of some spouses in Church callings can be difficult. Many of the members of the General Relief Society, Young Women, and Primary Presidencies have spouses. I have been impressed as I have had opportunities to observe how these men rally around and support their wives in their priesthood responsibilities. Perhaps as we recognize that the role of anyone involved in the Church is to help individuals and families gain eternal life, it is not so important who has the calling, but what each of us can do in our respective roles to make sure God's work and glory does come to pass. Perhaps one of the best things a stake president's wife can do is support her husband. Perhaps one of the best things a Relief Society president's husband can do is support his wife.

I am personally grateful for a husband who supports, discusses, and gives feedback, but who never is jealous or demeaning in any way of any of my roles. I'm confident he feels the same way about me. At the same time, we recognize that some callings, including those of bishop or Relief Society president, require confidentiality in such cases as transgression, worthiness, callings, and so forth, circumstances that would not be appropriate for us to share with each other. We do not push, pry, or take offense when confidential matters are wisely kept confidential. We work together as a team, he in his calling and me in mine, both striving to build the kingdom of God on earth.

## Women Have Great Influence on Men in How They Perform Their Callings

President Nelson shared an experience of interviewing a couple, "Carla and Carl," for the purpose of possibly calling the husband to be a mission president in a foreign land. As he did so, he explained that "Carla could feel Carl's fright as he began to shrink in his seat and express doubts about his capacity. While placing any of her own fears aside, Carla interrupted, saying, 'Carl, you can do whatever they ask of you.' Then she turned to me and said, 'He is a righteous man. He knows how to receive revelation. The Lord will help him, and I will stand beside him 100 percent.'" President Nelson explained that they completed their mission with success in a "faraway place."

President Nelson distilled the experience into this statement of principle: "With the help of the Lord and a supportive wife, a man can do infinitely more than he could ever do without that support."[10] As women, regardless of our marital status, we can support those who hold the priesthood by sustaining them, believing in them, fulfilling our callings, speaking well of them, and treating them as holders of God's priesthood here on earth.

## ADDITIONAL PRINCIPLES AND PRACTICES OF WOMEN AT CHURCH

Often, because priesthood power is so frequently associated with priesthood ordination, priesthood power is discussed in context of only men. In their book *The Melchizedek Priesthood,* Elder and Sister Renlund teach, however, that "women gain access to the power and blessings of God through receiving priesthood ordinances and making covenants."[11] Priesthood power comes through righteousness. Quoting President Joseph Fielding Smith, President Nelson recently reminded the women of the Church that "they have been given power and authority to do a great many things. The work which they do is done by divine authority."[12] In the same talk, President Nelson pled with the sisters of the Church: "We, your brethren, need your strength, your conversion, your conviction, your ability to lead, your wisdom, and your voices. The kingdom of God is not and cannot be complete without women who make sacred covenants and then keep them, women who can speak with the power and authority of God!"[13] Women, therefore, increase in priesthood power by making and keeping sacred covenants with God.

## The Church Was Not Fully Restored Until the Relief Society Was Organized

In March 1842, the Lord inspired the Prophet Joseph Smith to organize the women of the Church "under the priesthood and after the pattern of the priesthood"[14] and to teach them how they would "come in possession of the privileges, blessings, and gifts of the Priesthood."[15] When Joseph Smith turned the key of the priesthood in the women's meeting held in the upstairs room of the Red Brick Store in Nauvoo, he, according to President Oaks, "made the Relief Society an official part of the Church and kingdom of God."[16] In fact, Joseph Smith stated that the women of the Church were organized after the organization that existed in Christ's Church anciently.[17] He then visited Relief Society frequently and at least six times taught the women the doctrine of the gospel, focusing particularly on priesthood, to prepare them to receive their endowment in the house of the Lord.

This opened to women new opportunities for receiving knowledge and intelligence from on high, such as through the temple ordinances that were soon to be instituted.[18] The Church was therefore not complete without the organization of the Relief Society, just as an eternal family is not complete without the covenant union of a worthy woman and a worthy man.

## Both Men and Women Are Needed in the Church

Sister Bonnie L. Oscarson declared: "All women need to see themselves as essential participants in the work of the priesthood. Women in this Church are presidents, counselors, teachers, members of councils, sisters, and mothers, and the kingdom of God cannot function unless we rise up and fulfill our duties with faith."[19] Both men and women are needed "to labor in [the Lord's] vineyard for the salvation of the souls of men" (Doctrine and Covenants 138:56). According to *Handbook 2*, "This work of salvation includes member missionary work, convert retention, activation of less-active members, temple and family history work, . . . teaching the gospel," and caring for the poor and needy.[20]

Too often it is taught that the saving of souls is a priesthood duty. It's a Relief Society responsibility as well. All of us, as baptized, covenant-keeping members of the Church, have a responsibility to help others come unto Christ. President Nelson recently reminded us that Israel cannot be gathered without the women of the Church. And President Boyd K. Packer declared, "However much priesthood power and authority the men may possess—however much wisdom and experience they may accumulate—the safety of the family, the integrity of the doctrine, the ordinances, the covenants, indeed the future of the Church, rests equally upon the women."[21] I find the phrase "rests equally upon the women" interesting and insightful. God's work and glory simply cannot be accomplished without a unified effort of men and women. This topic of unity will be discussed in more detail later in this book.

> "All women need to see themselves as essential participants in the work of the priesthood. Women in this Church are presidents, counselors, teachers, members of councils, sisters, and mothers, and the kingdom of God cannot function unless we rise up and fulfill our duties with faith."
>
> —Bonnie L. Oscarson

## The Lord Has Never Explained Why Women Are Not Ordained to the Priesthood

President Oaks, on a number of occasions, has cautioned members of the Church to avoid answering questions the Lord has never given answers to: "Let's don't make the mistake that's been made in the past . . . trying to put reasons to revelation. The reasons turn out to be man-made to a great extent. The revelations are what we sustain as the will of the Lord and that's where safety lies."[22] President Ballard displayed a perfect example of this when he taught: "Why are men ordained to priesthood offices and not women? . . . The Lord has not revealed why He has organized His Church as He has."[23]

Although there is much we do know about women and the priesthood, there is much we still do not know. No man-made answer can answer that which God has never revealed. On the other hand, God has revealed so much in our dispensation on this topic and will continue to do so through His prophets and through personal revelation. As we continue to ask questions, ponder, and study the truths regarding the priesthood, we will be better prepared to live up to our privileges and help others whom we have been given authority and power to bless.

Chapter 4

# THE TEMPLE AND THE PATRIARCHAL ORDER OF THE PRIESTHOOD

Recently a student of mine explained that she had gone to the temple enough to have every word of the endowment memorized. She couldn't understand, therefore, why the Lord, through His prophets, would exhort us to return so often. In response to her question, I shared an experience President Boyd K. Packer had with President David O. McKay shortly before President McKay passed away. President Packer remembers President McKay speaking to General Authorities in the temple about sacred ordinances, explaining them and even quoting "at length from the ceremonies." In this setting, President McKay "paused and stood gazing up to the ceiling in deep thought." After being in this position for a time, he then declared, "Brethren, I think I am finally beginning to understand." President Packer reflected, "Here he was, the prophet—an Apostle for over half a century and even then, he was learning, he was growing."[1]

I admit that over the years there have been times when I too have found myself wondering what more there is to learn. However, through study, experience, and divine mentoring, I have come to understand that I am barely scraping the surface of what the Lord has to teach in His temples. President Packer taught that, in the temples, "we are continually instructed and enlightened on matters of spiritual importance. It comes line upon line, precept upon precept, until we gain a fullness of light and knowledge."[2]

In recent years I have focused my attention on the role of women in the temple: how the ordinances apply to women, what power and authority women receive in the temple, and how the patriarchal order of the priesthood found in the temple and in the earlier days of the earth's existence is similar to yet different from the hierarchical priesthood structure of the Church. I have found that as I have studied priesthood-related scriptures, followed the admonition of our leaders to memorize the oath and covenant of the priesthood, and learned more about the power and authority women receive in the temple, my temple experience has been enhanced tremendously. I have come to understand in part, perhaps, what President Spencer W. Kimball taught: "It wouldn't be far to crawl [to the temple] if one knew what [she] was getting and what [she] was missing if [she] didn't go."[3]

Because of the sacredness of the temple, many covenant members of the Church are reluctant to talk about it. "As a consequence," President Ezra Taft Benson cautioned, "many do not develop a real desire to go to the temple, or when they go there, they do so without much background to prepare them for the obligations and covenants they enter into."[4] Therefore, in this chapter, we will discuss the purpose, history, ordinances, and covenants of the patriarchal order of the priesthood (or new and everlasting covenant) as found in the temple, relying heavily on the scriptures and the published teachings of the prophets of the Church, taking care to keep sacred things sacred. By doing so, we will not only respect the holiness of the temple but also be better prepared to help ourselves and others take advantage of our priesthood privileges, understand and place our families in their rightful order, and participate as the Lord desires in the gathering of Israel.

## HISTORY OF THE PRIESTHOOD
## AND TEMPLE IN THIS DISPENSATION

Referring to the patriarchal order of the priesthood, the Prophet Joseph Smith admonished the Saints: "Go to and Finish the [Nauvoo] temple, and God will fill it with power, and you will then receive more knowledge concerning this Priesthood."⁵ Prior to the completion of the Nauvoo Temple, Joseph declared that God "has begun to restore the ancient order of His kingdom unto His servants and His people." In testifying of the fulfillment of the promise given of the Lord, he continued, "All things are concurring to bring about the completion of the fullness of the Gospel, a fullness of the dispensation of dispensations, even the fullness of times . . . to prepare the earth for the return of His glory, even a celestial glory, and a kingdom of Priests and kings to God and the Lamb, forever, on Mount Zion."⁶

Like Moses of old, Joseph Smith "sought diligently to sanctify his people that they might behold the face of God."⁷ In both ancient and modern times, sanctification was to be accomplished through the authority and ordinances of the patriarchal/familial order of the priesthood, the highest order of the Melchizedek Priesthood, and it was to be done only in the temple. Joseph explained, "The Church is not fully organized, in its proper order, and cannot be, until the Temple is completed."⁸ In other words, the Church could not be fully restored, with all of the rites and privileges granted in the days of Adam through Moses, without a temple on the earth to make that possible.

> The Church could not be fully restored, with all of the rites and privileges granted in the days of Adam through Moses, without a temple on the earth to make that possible.

It seems that both the Lord and Joseph were anxious to bestow the ordinances and authority of the patriarchal/familial order, for on May 4, 1842, the sacred ritual of the temple endowment was initiated as nine men met with the Prophet in the upper room of his store. "In this council," wrote the Prophet, "was instituted the ancient order of things for the first time in these last days," including "washings, anointings, endowments and the communication of keys pertaining to the Aaronic Priesthood, and so on to the highest order of the Melchizedek Priesthood . . . and all those plans and principles by which anyone is enabled to secure the fullness of those blessings which have been prepared for the Church of the First Born, and come up and abide in the presence of the Elohim in the eternal worlds."[9] Even though the Aaronic and Melchizedek Priesthoods had been restored some thirteen years before, it seems that the ordinances associated with the patriarchal/familial order of the priesthood—or the highest order of the Melchizedek Priesthood—available only in temples, were necessary for exaltation.

It wasn't just to the men, however, that these "washings, anointings, endowments and the communication of keys" were to be revealed in the patriarchal order. As part of the preparation for the temple ordinances, Joseph Smith in 1842 organized the Relief Society to serve as a "counterpart and companion to the men's priesthood quorums"[10]—both essential to the organization of the Church, and both necessary for the salvation of souls. On March 30, 1842, Joseph "instructed members of the newly organized Relief Society regarding their important role in the 'kingdom of Priests and kings,' the 'holy nation' which would be established as the Saints were endowed through temple ordinances."[11]

More than half a century later, in 1905, then-Relief Society General President Bathsheba W. Smith, who was present at the meetings conducted by Joseph Smith, commented on the Prophet's instructions to the women. "He said . . . he wanted to make us, as the women were in Paul's day, 'A kingdom of priestesses.' We have the ceremony in our endowments as Joseph taught."[12] Joseph, therefore, used the Relief Society to help prepare women to enter the temple, receive their own endowments, and enter into the patriarchal order.

In September 1843, the first women received their endowments. Unlike in the hierarchical priesthood structure, in the patriarchal structure of the temple, women performed sacred priesthood ordinances as they washed, anointed, and blessed each other and ministered in the holy endowment.[13] For the first time in this dispensation, men and women had the priesthood "conferred" upon them.[14] Using the keys revealed through Elijah, women and men were able to receive all the ordinances necessary to return, as families, to live with and like their Heavenly Parents forever in the eternal patriarchal/familial order.

# THE TEMPLE AND THE PATRIARCHAL ORDER OF THE PRIESTHOOD

## ESSENTIAL PURPOSE OF THE TEMPLE

President Russell M. Nelson expanded on the importance of temple ordinances in regard to exaltation when he taught: "The ordinances of the temple symbolize our reconciliation with the Lord and seal families together forever. Obedience to the sacred covenants of the temple qualifies us for eternal life, which is the glory of God."[15] How is the fulness of the priesthood received in the temple, and what are these associated ordinances that qualify us for eternal life? Elder Bruce R. McConkie taught that "this fulness is received through washings, anointings, solemn assemblies, oracles in holy places, conversations, ordinances, endowments, and sealings. (D&C 124:40.) It is in the temple that we enter into the patriarchal order, the order of priesthood that bears the name 'the new and everlasting covenant of marriage.'"[16] Therefore, each covenant a woman or man individually makes in the temple is part of the process of entering into the patriarchal/familial order, otherwise known as the new and everlasting covenant. Whether married or single, each woman or man therefore is individually receiving promised priesthood privileges and blessings associated with the patriarchal order of the priesthood or new and everlasting covenant.

## TEMPLE ORDINANCES

Since the temple is the Lord's house, all that we do in the temple—every covenant we make and every ordinance we participate in—reminds us of, is symbolic of, draws us closer to, and helps us become more like Jesus Christ. As stated earlier, the making and keeping of covenants associated with each ordinance, coupled with the Atonement of Jesus Christ, permits us to return to live with and become like our Heavenly Parents in the eternal family order. The moment a man begins making covenants, he starts the process of becoming a patriarch. The moment a woman begins making covenants, she starts the process of becoming a matriarch. Every ordinance leads them to the fulfillment of this great patriarchal/familial order of the priesthood. Baptism, the gift of the Holy Ghost, the Melchizedek Priesthood conferred upon men, the initiatory, and the endowment all lead up to the final ordinance, the sealing ordinance. Each ordinance gives additional power, blessings, understanding, intelligence, and light to each individual. Each draws us closer, as women and men, to becoming like our Heavenly Mother and Father.

All of the temple ordinances are separate and distinct and include covenants made between the individual and the Lord. Unlike in the administration of the hierarchical priesthood structure, both men and women have authority to perform priesthood ordinances in the temple. President M. Russell Ballard taught: "All who enter the house of the Lord officiate in the ordinances of the priesthood. This applies to men and women alike."[17] Interestingly enough, although men must be ordained to the priesthood in order to enter the temple and perform these ordinances, women do not.

## The Initiatory (Washings and Anointings)

The Lord, in Doctrine and Covenants 88:74, invites those members of the Church who are entering the temple to "cleanse your hands and your feet before me." The initiatory ordinance provides this opportunity for both men and women in preparation for other sacred temple ordinances. This ordinance signifies "the cleansing and sanctifying power of Jesus Christ applied to the attributes of the person and the hallowing of all life."[18] As was the case with Adam and Eve, Abraham and Sarah, and all other couples and individuals who have received sacred temple ordinances, a sacred priesthood garment is given to covenant members to be worn during their lives as a symbol and reminder of the covenants made with and blessings promised by the Lord.[19] It is important to note that following these sacred ordinances, both women and men are provided temple clothing to remind them of their covenants.[20] Reflecting on the promises and blessings associated with this ordinance, Elder Robert D. Hales declared that they "are worthy of great contemplation and provide incredible power and protection." He continued: "When we enter the house of the Lord, the ordinances and the Spirit that attends us sanctify our souls. This sanctification begins with the initiatory ordinances of washing and anointing. These are preparatory ordinances. They provide the cleanliness and purification we need to receive the endowment."[21]

Just as in the days of Moses, when the sons of Aaron were brought before the "door of the tabernacle" (Exodus 29:4) to be prepared to enter the temple, so are worthy members, both male and female, who desire to make covenants with the Lord today. We do not know whether women participated in this early ordinance, but there is no question that women are washed and anointed today. The oath and covenant of the priesthood, as explained in Doctrine and Covenants 84, seems to allude to this very moment, as there is a preparation and cleansing taking place. Virginia Pearce, quoting Andrew F. Ehat and Lyndon Cook, teaches that "in the Temple women would with oil and by the laying on of hands confer on their sisters blessings."[22] Thus, as President Ballard taught, women both receive and perform sacred priesthood ordinances in the temple—ordinances necessary for exaltation—starting with the initiatory.[23]

## Endowment

The endowment, according to Brigham Young, is "to receive all those ordinances in the house of the Lord, which are necessary for you, after you have departed this life, to enable you to walk back to the presence of the Father, passing the angels who stand as sentinels . . . and gain your eternal exaltation."[24] During the endowment, instruction is given regarding premortal life, the Creation, the Fall, and the laws and ordinances made available through the Atonement of Jesus Christ, which are required for repentance and eternal life.[25] In the endowment, members covenant and promise to be obedient and chaste and, according to Elder James E. Talmage, "to be charitable, benevolent, tolerant and pure; to devote both talent and material means to the spread of truth and the uplifting of the [human] race; to maintain devotion to the cause of truth; and to seek in every way to contribute to the great preparation that the earth may be made ready to receive Jesus Christ."[26]

In the endowment ordinance, both men and women wear the "robes of the holy priesthood."[27] Regarding this ordinance, Brigham Young also taught that "the Priesthood is given to the people . . . and, when properly understood, they may actually unlock the treasury of the Lord, and receive to their fullest satisfaction."[28] Sheri Dew surmises: "Surely the 'treasury of the Lord' includes the 'wonders of eternity' and the 'riches of eternity' that the Lord wishes to give His sons and daughters. Surely it includes the 'mysteries of God' that are granted unto those who give Him heed and diligence."[29] This treasury of the Lord and these mysteries of God enable both men and women to be filled with great power as their eyes are opened as to how to access and use God's power in His prescribed manner.

In the endowment, both women and men perform and receive priesthood ordinances, and both men and women are instructed on how to use priesthood authority and power. In fact, President Nelson declared, "We need women . . . who understand the power and peace of the temple endowment."[30] As women, therefore, it is not good enough to know that the power of God exists, or even to have a testimony of it, but we must understand the doctrine of it, access it, and use it.

Elder James E. Talmage taught an interesting truth in regard to the authority of the priesthood women receive in the temple. He stated, "Women of the Church share the authority of the Priesthood with their husbands, actual or prospective." Elder Talmage's careful use of the term *prospective* seems to indicate that although marriage is necessary for women to share the authority of the priesthood, it does not need to happen prior to its reception. God, who is not limited by time, gives the blessings to worthy, covenant-keeping women regardless of their current marital status. Elder Talmage goes on to explain that although women are not ordained to a specific rank in the priesthood, "there is no grade, rank, or phase of the temple endowment to which women are not eligible on an equality with men."[31] In no way does this minimize the importance of marriage, which is clearly necessary for exaltation, as will be described in the next section. It does, however, help all women understand the blessings and privileges associated with the covenants made in the temple and the power and authority that go with them outside of those sacred temple walls. If priesthood authority and power received in the temple are shared between a husband and wife, it seems logical that they both possess it for the purposes taught in the temple.

Elder Talmage concludes his thoughts on the sharing of priesthood authority between wives and husbands by declaring: "The married state is regarded as sacred, sanctified, and holy in all temple procedure; and within the House of the Lord the woman is the equal and the help-meet of the man. In the privileges and blessings of that holy place, the utterance of Paul is regarded as a scriptural decree in full force and effect: 'Neither is the man without the woman, neither the woman without the man, in the Lord.'"[32]

## Sealing

The culminating ordinance of the temple, therefore, is the sealing ordinance, which binds a family together now and for eternity. President Joseph Fielding Smith taught: "If you want salvation in the fullest, that is exaltation in the kingdom of God, so that you may become his sons and his daughters, you have got to go into the temple.... No man shall receive ... that blessing alone; but man and wife, when they receive the sealing power in the temple of the Lord, ... shall pass on to exaltation, and shall continue and become like the Lord."[33] Indeed, the greatest blessings of the temple—those required for exaltation, those that directly lead to us becoming like our Heavenly Parents—are not received alone. They are possible and available only with a covenant made between a woman and a man in the sealing ordinance.

The Lord, through the Prophet Joseph Smith, taught that there are "three heavens or degrees" in the celestial glory, and "in order to obtain the highest, a man must enter into this order of the priesthood [meaning the new and everlasting covenant of marriage]; and if he does not, he cannot obtain it" (Doctrine and Covenants 131:1–3). This new and everlasting covenant of marriage is made by both woman and man as part of the sealing ordinance, and by so covenanting, the couple together enters into the patriarchal/familial order of the priesthood. Elder Cree-L Kofford, emeritus member of the Seventy, taught that the new and everlasting covenant of marriage is another way of saying "patriarchal order." Elder Kofford continued, "Thus, that portion of section 131 could read: 'And in order to obtain the highest, a man must enter into the patriarchal order of the priesthood.'"[34]

With the keys revealed by Elijah, held only by the Apostles, the blessings of Abraham, Isaac, and Jacob are pronounced upon this eternal couple (see Doctrine and Covenants 84:33–40; 132:19; Abraham 2:11). With a man and a woman kneeling on equal level, opposite each other, with a sacred altar in the middle, they enter mutually into the new and everlasting covenant with each other and the Lord. They thus begin a new family kingdom as husband and wife in the patriarchal order. Through this sealing ordinance, "the family unit will continue, and they will gain the highest reward and the greatest honor and glory that our Father can bestow on any of his children. They will be gods, even the sons of God, and all things will be theirs, for they will receive of the fulness of the Father."[35]

Therefore, together as wife and husband they become joint-inheritors of all that the Father has. Both man and woman receive exaltation and eternal life together. Both man and woman thus have the potential to become gods together. Doctrine and Covenants 132:20 teaches: "Then shall they be gods, because they have no end; therefore shall they be from everlasting to everlasting, because they continue; then shall they be above all, because all things are subject unto them. Then shall they be gods, because they have all power, and the angels are subject unto them."

This new and everlasting covenant of marriage, which formally invites the couple as husband and wife into the patriarchal order, is available only in the temple. It is the eternal structure of the family after the order of our Heavenly Parents. Godhood, therefore, is for women and men together. The making of the covenant is the beginning, but living according to the covenant—working, sacrificing, becoming Christlike—is critical in order to have the ordinance ratified by the Holy Spirit of Promise, and for both woman and man to reach their full potential. Elder and Sister Dale G. and Ruth L. Renlund explain:

> Only through the sealing ordinances of the holy Melchizedek Priesthood, performed in the temple of the Lord and ratified by the Holy Spirit of Promise, and through faithful, righteous living can a man and a woman join in an eternal marriage unit wherein they may attain a fulness of the priesthood and exaltation together (see Doctrine and Covenants 132:18–19). All blessings, benefits, and inheritances of the Melchizedek Priesthood are equally shared and achieved by husband and wife if they keep their covenants and live in love, harmony, and cooperation in the Lord.[36]

In fact, as wife and husband enter into this new and everlasting covenant, or the patriarchal order, and live according to the associated covenants, they become an eternal house of Israel.[37] Their children, now "born in the covenant," thus become a part of that eternal house.

## Vicarious Ordinances for the Dead

In addition to the temple ordinances performed for the living, these and additional ordinances are performed vicariously for those who have passed beyond the veil. Elder John A. Widtsoe spoke incredible words in this regard: "Once only may a person receive the temple endowment for himself, but innumerable times may he receive it for those gone from the earth. Whenever he does so, he performs an unselfish act for which no earthly recompense is available. He tastes in part the sweet joy of saviorhood. He rises toward the stature of the Lord Jesus Christ who died for all."[38]

This opportunity for us to perform ordinances, especially for family members and loved ones now deceased, is not only one of the greatest opportunities provided for covenant members; it also provides a salvific service for those to whom we owe a great debt, allowing them to enter into the patriarchal order of the priesthood and thus dwell eternally in our Heavenly Parents' family. The performing of these ordinances is a significant part of the gathering of Israel. Those who perform these ordinances in behalf of people on the other side of the veil are literally saviors for those who are unable to do the work for themselves. Indeed, they without us and we without them cannot be saved. In a stirring talk to new members of the Church, President Henry B. Eyring explained: "When you were baptized, your ancestors looked down on you with hope. Perhaps after centuries, they rejoiced to see one of their descendants make a covenant to find them and to offer them freedom. In your reunion, you will see in their eyes either gratitude or terrible disappointment. Their hearts are bound to you. Their hope is in your hands."[39] Whether we are recent converts or converts whose families have been in the Church for generations, all of us have family whose "hope is in [our] hands."

In order for vicarious work for those who have passed beyond the veil to lead to exaltation, both men and women must perform and receive sacred ordinances in their behalf. For, once again, neither a man nor a woman can receive exaltation without the other. Perhaps this is in part what President Nelson meant when he declared: "My dear sisters, we need *you*! . . . We simply cannot gather Israel without you."[40] In fact, according to the government of the Lord, it is impossible to do so.

## PRIESTHOOD AUTHORITY, KEYS, AND POWER IN THE TEMPLE

Just as priesthood ordination is not required for women to perform sacred priesthood functions in the temple, as it is in the hierarchical structure of the priesthood, priesthood authority, keys, and power also have unique conditions in the temple.

### Priesthood Authority in the Temple

When members of the Church are baptized and later partake of the ordinance of the sacrament, they covenant with the Lord that they are willing to take upon them the name of Jesus Christ. It is in the temple that they literally take upon themselves the name of Christ, both women and men alike. This willingness to take upon ourselves the name of Jesus Christ, according to President Dallin H. Oaks, "can therefore be understood as willingness to take upon us the *authority* of Jesus Christ. . . . By partaking of the sacrament we witness our willingness to participate in the sacred ordinances of the temple and to receive the highest blessings available through the *name* and by the *authority* of the Savior."[41]

Thus, when women and men enter the temple to receive their endowments, they receive the authority to act in the name of Jesus Christ in their personal lives and in their families. Listening to the teachings in the initiatory and endowment will help clarify what priesthood authority is available to both men and women in the temple. Elder Bruce R. McConkie taught, "Where spiritual things are concerned, as pertaining to all of the gifts of the Spirit, with reference to the receipt of revelation, the gaining of testimonies, and the seeing of visions, in all matters that pertain to godliness and holiness and which are brought to pass as a result of personal righteousness—in all these things men and women stand in a position of absolute equality before the Lord."[42]

> When women and men enter the temple to receive their endowments, they receive the authority to act in the name of Jesus Christ in their personal lives and in their families. Listening to the teachings in the initiatory and endowment will help clarify what priesthood authority is available to both men and women in the temple.

## Priesthood Keys in the Temple

Priesthood keys perform a different function in the temple than in the hierarchical structure of the Church. There are three common uses of the term *key* in regard to the temple. First, there are the apostolic keys, which allow for the sealing of families for eternity. Second, the keys held by the temple president ensure that ordinances are performed correctly. The third keys are the keys of knowledge and wisdom.

Brigham Young taught, "The keys of the eternal priesthood, which is after the order of the Son of God, is comprehended by being an apostle. All the priesthood, all the keys, all the gifts, all the endowments and everything preparatory to entering back into the presence of the Father and of the Son, is composed of, circumscribed by, or I might say incorporated within the circumference of the apostleship."[43] As stated in *Handbook 2*, only certain of the keys held by apostles and prophets are delegated. Those keys pertaining to sealings are held strictly by the Apostles and are used only under the direction of the First Presidency.[44] Temple sealers do not hold keys of sealing but rather are authorized to perform sealings under the authority of the First Presidency.

The keys that govern the temple are those keys revealed through Elijah the prophet to Joseph Smith and Oliver Cowdery in the Kirtland Temple. The keys revealed by Elijah, President Boyd K. Packer taught, "hold sufficient authority to perform all of the ordinances necessary to redeem and to exalt the whole human family. And, because we have the keys to the sealing power, what we bind in proper order here will be bound in heaven. Those keys—the keys to seal and bind on earth, and have it bound in heaven—represent the consummate gift from our God. With that authority we can baptize and bless, we can endow and seal, and the Lord will honor our commitments."[45] These are the apostolic keys related to the temple.

The second keys are those held by the temple president. Often misunderstood, the priesthood keys held by the temple president are for the purposes of making sure the ordinances are done correctly—they are not sealing keys. Temple presidents and temple sealers are authorized to perform sealings under the authority of the key holders, who are the First Presidency. President Packer taught that just as there are limits to the keys held by those who are ordained to priesthood offices in the Church, "special authorization" must be given for men and women to perform priesthood functions in the temple.[46]

The third keys primarily referred to in the temple are the keys of the "mysteries of the kingdom, even the key of the knowledge of God" (Doctrine and Covenants 84:19). These keys could otherwise be known as rights or privileges, not to be confused with priesthood keys of presidency, as discussed in the previous chapter. In Doctrine and Covenants 84:19–22, the Lord explains, "And this greater priesthood administereth the gospel and holdeth the key of the mysteries of the kingdom, even the key of the knowledge of God. Therefore, in the ordinances thereof, the power of godliness is manifest. And without the ordinances thereof, and the authority of the priesthood, the power of godliness is not manifest unto men in the flesh; for without this no man can see the face of God, even the Father, and live." In other words, through the Melchizedek Priesthood, all worthy temple-covenant-making and covenant-keeping members, male and female, are able to receive "the mysteries of the kingdom, even the key of the knowledge of God" through the temple endowment. In fact, using this scripture passage as a reference, President Nelson shared his concern that "too many of our brothers and sisters do not fully understand the concept of priesthood power and authority," and that they "do not grasp the privileges that could be theirs."[47]

To know the mysteries of God and to have the knowledge of God! What greater mysteries and knowledge could we want? To be the recipients of the power of godliness through the ordinances of the gospel, performed in the temple, by both men and women? No other power is greater than the power of godliness. To be able to see the face of God, even the Father, and live!

In addition to section 84, President Nelson also referenced Doctrine and Covenants 107:18–19, which specifies even more privileges for both men and women associated with these keys: "The power and authority of the higher, or Melchizedek Priesthood, is to hold the keys of all the spiritual blessings of the church—to have the privilege of receiving the mysteries of the kingdom of heaven, to have the heavens opened unto them, to commune with the general assembly and church of the Firstborn, and to enjoy the communion and presence of God the Father, and Jesus the mediator of the new covenant."

Traditionally, sections 84 and 107 of the Doctrine and Covenants are known as priesthood sections, and no distinction is made between the hierarchical and patriarchal orders of the priesthood. Therefore, often, the blessings and priesthood privileges mentioned in these sections are used in the context of the hierarchical priesthood structure and applied to men only. A more thorough reading of these sections, in the broader context of Church history, helps us to understand that these promises apply to the patriarchal order of the priesthood used in the temple. Therefore, *they apply to all who make covenants in the Lord's holy house.* Elder M. Russell Ballard quoted Elder John A. Widtsoe as saying: "The Priesthood is for the benefit of all members of the Church. Men have no greater claim than women upon the blessings that issue from the Priesthood and accompany its possession."[48] I find it fascinating that he even adds "accompany its possession," meaning perhaps that not only do men and women receive the blessings of the priesthood, but a man, just because he is ordained to a priesthood office, does not have blessings given to him that a righteous woman cannot have.

Besides the enhanced ability to have this wisdom and knowledge for themselves, covenant-keeping women are blessed and admonished to use this knowledge and wisdom in the home, especially in the nurturing of children. Although the concept is sometimes misunderstood, the temple shows, and modern-day prophets have clearly taught, that women can speak directly with God. In fact, to the Relief Society sisters of his day, as he was preparing them for the temple, the Prophet Joseph Smith explained, "If you live up to your privileges, the angels cannot be restrain'd from being your associates—females, if they are pure and innocent can come into the presence of God."[49]

## Power from Ordinances

"Our Father in Heaven is generous with His power," President Ballard declared. "All men and all women have access to this power for help in our own lives."[50] As a reminder, God's power is priesthood. Priesthood power, or God's power, is gained by an individual in the temple as a gift from Him, primarily in two ways: through ordinances and through righteousness. In discussing the power that comes through making covenants in the temple, Elder D. Todd Christofferson instructed: "Our access to that power is through our covenants with Him. . . . In all the ordinances, especially those of the temple, we are endowed with power from on high."[51] Elder Tad R. Callister, then of the Seventy, taught that the ordinances of the temple are more than something we do to satisfy the demands to enter into the celestial kingdom, but rather, "they are the keys that open the doors to heavenly powers that can lift us above our mortal limitations."[52]

Not only is power received in the temple, but, according to President George Q. Cannon, "Every foundation stone that is laid for a temple, and every temple completed according to the order the Lord has revealed for His holy priesthood, lessens the power of Satan on the earth, and increases the power of God and godliness, moves the heavens in mighty power in our behalf, invokes and calls down upon us the blessings of eternal gods, and those who reside in their presence."[53]

## Power from Righteousness

Whether the structure of priesthood government is hierarchical or patriarchal, the power of heaven available to individuals is dependent upon their righteousness. We know that worthiness is central to performing and receiving priesthood ordinances. Sister Linda K. Burton, former Relief Society General President, correctly taught, "Righteousness is the qualifier . . . to invite priesthood power into our lives."[54] Therefore, as women, we truly do receive priesthood power as we make and keep temple covenants and live righteously in accordance with those covenants.

## Blessings of Temple Work

The blessings and joy of the temple are, according to President Nelson, "beyond our present comprehension."[55] President Thomas S. Monson stated: "Until you have entered the house of the Lord and have received all the blessings which await you there, you have not obtained everything the Church has to offer. The all-important and crowning blessings of membership in the Church are those blessings which we receive in the temples of God."[56] President Gordon B. Hinckley declared, "I believe that no member of the Church has received the ultimate which this Church has to give until he or she has received his or her temple blessings in the house of the Lord."[57]

Frankly, the blessings of the temple are innumerable. Some of these blessings are associated with promises made by the Father to His children; some of these blessings are received individually, one miracle, one piece of knowledge, or one answer to prayer at a time. Rather than enumerating all the blessings of the temple, I simply invite you to study what the Brethren and general auxiliary leaders have said on this topic. In addition, I invite you to ponder on the blessings you have received, or the blessings you are personally aware of that have been granted to those you know. President Ballard taught that those who make and keep temple covenants will be blessed to "receive personal revelation, to be blessed by the ministering of angels, to commune with God, to receive the fulness of the gospel," and, he added, to ultimately "become heirs alongside Jesus Christ of all our Father has."[58] There simply is not more that God could give.

Sister Carol F. McConkie of the Young Women General Presidency invited us to "come to the temple and be sealed in eternal family relationships. Come to the temple and receive heavenly power. Come to the temple, and know that you enter His house and feel His presence there. Come to the temple to be purified and prepared to see God's face and to know that He lives." She then testified that "as we come to the temple, we will know who we are and what we are here for, what we are to do, and where we are going. We will receive answers to our prayers and receive revelation."[59]

## Blessings of Temple Attendance with Family History and Vicarious Work for the Dead

While walking to my car in the underground parking garage of the Church Office Building a few years ago, I saw President Russell M. Nelson also walking to his car. Though he did not know me at all, he raised his hand, which held temple name cards, and expressed what a great day it was, as he had just accomplished the work for some of his own ancestors. President Nelson taught that "genealogical research and temple service are one work in this Church." He continued, "Neither stands alone. Together, they enable eternal exaltation for our kindred. Elijah's mission caused the hearts of the children to be turned to their fathers. That same Elijah conferred keys of priesthood authority that allow families to be sealed together forever. Indeed, genealogical research and temple service are one work in this church."[60]

Elder Dale G. Renlund compiled a long list of blessings that are promised to those who participate in both family history and temple work. It seems that in our day and age, with so much confusion, negativity, frustration, fear, doubt, despair, and temptation, these blessings are worthy of our every effort:

- Increased understanding of the Savior and His atoning sacrifice;
- Increased influence of the Holy Ghost to feel strength and direction for our own lives;
- Increased faith, so that conversion to the Savior becomes deep and abiding;
- Increased ability and motivation to learn and repent because of an understanding of who we are, where we come from, and a clearer vision of where we are going;
- Increased refining, sanctifying, and moderating influences in our hearts;
- Increased joy through an increased ability to feel the love of the Lord;
- Increased family blessings, no matter our current, past, or future family situation or how imperfect our family tree may be;
- Increased love and appreciation for ancestors and living relatives, so we no longer feel alone;
- Increased power to discern that which needs healing and thus, with the Lord's help, serve others;
- Increased protection from temptations and the intensifying influence of the adversary; and
- Increased assistance to mend troubled, broken, or anxious hearts and make the wounded whole.[61]

I do not believe there is a person on this earth who could not benefit from these promised blessings. Additional blessings were declared by President Nelson in his first message as President of the Church: "Your worship in the temple and your service there for your ancestors will bless you with increased personal revelation and peace and will fortify your commitment to stay on the covenant path."[62] As I have talked with temple-covenant-keeping Latter-day Saints, young and old, male and female, lifelong member and recent convert, it has become clear to me that this promise from President Nelson is real. In a similar manner, Elder John A. Widtsoe explained that when any person does vicarious work for another, he reviews the teachings and is reminded of his own covenants with God. "His memory is refreshed, his conscience warned, his hopes lifted heavenward. Temple repetition is the mother of daily blessings. Wherever one turns, temple service profits those who perform it."[63]

## CONCLUSION

I recently sat with a number of members of the Community of Christ, previously known as the Reorganized Church of Jesus Christ of Latter Day Saints, as part of an interfaith dialogue. I have great love and respect for these people, those I consider brothers and sisters in the faith. We talked openly and in a friendly manner about similarities and differences between our two churches and landed squarely on the topic of women and the priesthood. One of the women in the room who had been ordained to the priesthood described her responsibilities and shared her feelings regarding the blessing it was for her to be able to perform priesthood ordinances.

Although the conversation was interesting and enlightening, it didn't take long for me to realize the paradox of the conversation. Here we were, women whose Church membership traced back to the same original Church established by God through the Prophet Joseph Smith. Due to decisions made after the death of the Prophet by early Church members who did not see eye to eye, perhaps especially in regard to priesthood authority, there was a division. Because of the direction taken by the leaders of the Reorganized Church, women were ordained to priesthood offices. I, however, due to revelation from God through His prophets, was not ordained to a priesthood office in the Church and therefore was not given the associated responsibilities. The result of this dialogue could have made me, as a Latter-day Saint woman, feel demeaned or insignificant. Yet I knew better, for I understood the priesthood power and authority with which I had been endowed in the temple.

The paradox, as I see it, is twofold: First, I believe I belong to the only true Church of Jesus Christ of Latter-day Saints, which therefore means I believe that only in this Church is the authority for anyone to act in the name of God present, valid, real, and of worth. Women in the Church, although not ordained to the priesthood, still act with legitimate priesthood power and authority in the ecclesiastical structure of the Church—authority that is not made available to any other women or men on the earth. So, paradoxically, though I hold no priesthood office, I believe I exercise more priesthood authority than do my sisters in other religious groups. The second paradox revolves around the significance of the temple. Members of the Community of Christ—or any other church, for that matter—do not have spiritual knowledge of, believe in, understand, or take part in the priesthood ordinances, covenants, promises, and blessings associated with and available only in the temple. Only covenant-making and covenant-keeping Latter-day Saint women and men have the power and authority and keys associated with the temple, as discussed previously. Only covenant-keeping Latter-day Saint women and men have the promises and perspective associated with the covenants made in the temple that bless us and others now and throughout eternity.

President Nelson invited all those who have received temple ordinances to labor together to bring these blessings to all members. "For members to fall short of that objective would be like paying for a banquet and then leaving after salad has been served. The sublime feast at the banquet table of opportunity in the Church is experienced in the temple. The ordinances therein constitute the ultimate reason for our membership in the Church."[64]

How much more could we want? How much more could the Father give than all that He has already given? The gift has been made available; it is our job to receive it and help others do the same.

Recently, I watched a UPS worker deliver a large and heavy box to the front porch of my neighbors' home the day before Christmas. Knowing the family was on vacation, I pushed the box up against the side of the house to protect it. I was surprised when, after a week, the box was still there although the family had returned from their vacation. The situation, as explained by my neighbor, was not only humorous, but poignant. The teenage son had been complaining the entire week since Christmas that he had not received the gift he had wanted. His snide remarks, ingratitude for the presents he had already been given, and "woe-is-me" demeanor were negatively affecting the family. During this same week, the parents were kindly asking the young man to bring in the box from outside. Complaining that the box was too heavy and the task too time consuming, unwilling to help his parents when they were so insensitive to his own needs, he refused to carry in the box. His long-waited-for and greatly desired gift was literally feet away, but, unwilling to accept the invitation of his parents, he remained upset and forsaken.

Like this young man, many of us do not realize the blessings that have already been given to us, the privileges that are already ours, and the gifts that are waiting to be bestowed for only a little effort on our part. If we knew what was only feet away, we couldn't run fast enough or crawl far enough to get it. I believe, as Elder Renlund so profoundly taught, as taught to him by Elder Wilford W. Andersen of the Seventy, that "the greater the distance between the giver and the receiver, the more the receiver develops a sense of entitlement."[65] The opposite, I believe, is also true: the closer we are to the Lord and His servants, the more grateful we are and the more willing we are to listen to and obey their counsel. Although I am far from perfect, as I have listened to the teachings of the prophets and the Spirit of the Lord and made and kept sacred covenants with Him, I too have come to "stand all amazed" at the love and grace offered to me by Jesus.[66] I simply cannot imagine receiving so much for so little. No sacrifice is too great. I believe that we, as members of the Church and especially as women, need to understand much more fully the doctrine of the priesthood, particularly the great blessings and privileges given all worthy members of the Church in the temple. The more we do so, the more we will be astounded and humbled by the blessings of the "ultimate Givers."[67]

# Chapter 5

# "ENDOWED WITH PRIESTHOOD POWER"

## Connecting Women with Priesthood in the Temple and Home

I recently had a conversation with a wonderful male colleague who asked why I was teaching about women and the priesthood in my Eternal Family class. I simply responded, "For the same reason I talk about men and the priesthood in my Eternal Family class. Priesthood applies to both! Knowing the truth regarding the priesthood, its use, power, blessings, and responsibilities, strengthens all of us as individuals and as families. Priesthood at its core is about families!" Imagine the strength, power, and authority a family would have if husband and wife, brothers and sisters all understood and used the priesthood in the way the Lord intended! Imagine what a difference it would make in the world if women of the Church truly understood their priesthood privileges and led their families and other women of the world using righteous principles and the power received through making and keeping sacred covenants.

Elder J Ballard Washburn of the Seventy stated: "We go to the temple to make covenants, but we go home to keep the covenants that we have made. The home is the testing ground. The home is the place where we learn to be more Christlike. The home is the place where we learn to overcome selfishness and give ourselves in service to others."[1]

The "home" referred to by Elder Washburn is likely different for many people. When I was growing up, my home was full of family:

siblings, nephews and nieces, parents, cousins, and so on. For most of my adult life, my home was an apartment or house shared with roommates, a place where I lived alone, or my parents' house, into which I moved to help care for my mother as she passed away, and subsequently to care for my father. Now my home is shared with my husband. He too was raised in a large family and was used to commotion and fun. Like me, he lived a single life for years, both with roommates and alone. Now the two of us, although our home often serves as a bed-and-breakfast for friends and family, live together in a much quieter home than either of us is accustomed to. We have wanted and tried to have children be a part of our family and home, but have been unable to. Through it all, we have striven to implement what we have learned in the temple, from the prophets and leaders of the Church, and from personal revelation into our homes and lives, both as individuals and now as a couple with the hope of having our own children someday.

Just as in the temple, the home is structured in the order of the patriarchal or family government. Whether single, divorced, married to an inactive member, widowed, married to an active member, or whatever our circumstances, we, as covenant-keeping women, are able to leave the temple with the authority, keys, and power of the temple to be used in our own homes and lives. We have been blessed with incredible priesthood privileges that, when understood and used according to the Lord's desire, will allow us to fill the measure of our creation during this time of our existence on the earth. In this chapter we will look at how to apply the priesthood privileges of the temple in our homes as we strive to place the home back in its primary place. There is a reason that only the home is as sacred as the temple.

In 2014, Sister Linda K. Burton, then serving as the Relief Society General President, challenged all women at the BYU Women's Conference to memorize the oath and covenant of the priesthood (Doctrine and Covenants 84:33–40) in order to help women better understand the priesthood.[2] Often, the oath and covenant of the priesthood is taught as if it were referring to the priesthood operating in the hierarchical structure of the Church. A closer look at the history of section 84 and its link to the temple will help us understand that it is likely the patriarchal priesthood that this oath and covenant is referring to. Therefore, the promises associated with the oaths and covenants entered into are for both women and men.

Imagine women making sacred covenants in the initiatory ordinance with this passage of the oath and covenant of the priesthood in their minds:

> For whoso is faithful unto the obtaining these two priesthoods of which I have spoken, and the magnifying their calling, are sanctified by the Spirit unto the renewing of their bodies.
>
> They become the sons of Moses and of Aaron and the seed of Abraham, and the church and kingdom, and the elect of God.
>
> And also all they who receive this priesthood receive me, saith the Lord;
>
> For he that receiveth my servants receiveth me;
>
> And he that receiveth me receiveth my Father;
>
> And he that receiveth my Father receiveth my Father's kingdom; therefore all that my Father hath shall be given unto him.
>
> And this is according to the oath and covenant which belongeth to the priesthood.
>
> Therefore, all those who receive the priesthood, receive this oath and covenant of my Father, which he cannot break, neither can it be moved. (Doctrine and Covenants 84:33–40)

After I had memorized the oath and covenant of the priesthood, as Sister Burton exhorted, and done initiatory ordinances with these words of the oath and covenant running through my mind, the connection finally clicked for me. Following President Russell M. Nelson's invitation to learn from the Lord, who "loves to do His own teaching in His holy house," and is pleased if we would ask Him to teach us "about priesthood keys, authority, and power as [we] experience the ordinances of the Melchizedek Priesthood in the holy temple,"[3] I felt as if my eyes were opened. For the first time, after having done initiatory work for over twenty years, I realized, in part, what the oath and covenant of the priesthood had to do with me—and it has changed my life. I strongly suggest that we follow the invitations of our Church leaders and strive to better understand the priesthood in a personal way only the Spirit can teach. I am absolutely convinced that there is much the Lord is trying to teach us, especially His daughters.

Imagine the strength given to covenant-keeping women to know that "all that [the] Father hath shall be given unto [them]." Imagine the peace and hope and joy this statement in and of itself gave to the early pioneer women who, as they left Nauvoo, looked back at their abandoned temple with the fire of this covenant burning in their hearts. Clearly, the Lord's timing was manifest when He had the women receive their temple endowments before crossing the plains. Imagine what a difference it makes for covenant-keeping women of all situations to know that in the future they are promised to receive "all that my Father hath," and that God has promised that He will "go before your face," that He "will be on your right hand and on your left," and that His "Spirit shall be in your hearts," and His "angels round about you, to bear you up" (Doctrine and Covenants 84:38, 88). Can we imagine the strength this truth gives to our single sisters, living away from home, working, in school, on missions, raising children, or living in their own homes as adult mature women, but with no male in the home who has been ordained to a priesthood office? Can we recognize the assurance this may give to a divorced woman or single mother who has made and continues to keep sacred temple covenants? I know for me, as a single sister until age forty, this knowledge of having God by my side and angels round about me was real and significant. I felt it. I knew it. It gave me peace when I was confused, comfort when I was alone, strength when I was weak, and faith when I questioned. In fact, after the passing of my mother, the idea of angels being around me became even more significant during many lonely years and situations. There were times when I knew without question that I was not alone, that angels indeed were around me.

Understanding how the oath and covenant of the priesthood and its associated blessings applied to women, my desire to better comprehend and apply other temple teachings in my own life and home increased. I began to realize, once again, that I was just scraping the surface of what the Lord was trying to teach me. But the more I learned, the more effective I could be and the greater impact for good I could have in my family and whatever else the Lord desired that I do. Recognizing that authority, keys, and power are essential components of the hierarchical structure of the Church, I felt it important to understand how these same components taught in the temple affected women and how the Lord intended women to use these truths in their individual lives and in their own homes.

## AUTHORITY, POWER, AND KEYS RECEIVED IN THE ENDOWMENT

### Authority Women Receive from the Temple for Our Personal Lives and for Our Families

Although it is not appropriate to speak of the actual authorities given to both men and women in the endowment, I would invite all those who have received their endowments in the temple to return, looking for how the Lord, through His servants, teaches women and men to use their priesthood authority. In fact, President M. Russell Ballard, after speaking of the strength of our pioneer ancestors, exhorted, "Like faithful sisters in the past, you need to learn how to use the priesthood authority with which you have been endowed to obtain every eternal blessing that will be yours." Then, like President Nelson, he told us that "today more than ever, we need faithful, dedicated sister-Saints who ... have hearts that are fixed, who trust in the Lord, and who 'with the fire of Israel's God burning in [their bosoms]' are willing to save souls and build the kingdom of God."[4] Women literally receive this priesthood authority directly from God in the temple.

### Power We Take from the Temple for Our Own Lives

All temple-covenant-keeping members are literally endowed with power. Sister Sheri Dew affirmed, "Endowed, covenant-keeping women have direct access to priesthood power for their own lives" (and, I would add, for those within their stewardship). "What does it mean to have access to priesthood power for our own lives?" Sister Dew asked. "It means that we can receive revelation, be blessed and aided by the ministering of angels, learn to part the veil that separates us from our Heavenly Father, be strengthened to resist temptation, be protected, and be enlightened and made smarter than we are—all without any mortal intermediary."⁵ In other words, although we do need husbands, brothers, and fathers as part of God's eternal plan, and we do appreciate the love and blessings given by those called to minister for us, a covenant-keeping sister can have the power of the priesthood in her home regardless of her marital status or the activity level of her husband. Sister Dew explained, "Men and women who are endowed in the house of the Lord have been given a gift of power, and they have been given a gift of knowledge to know how to access and use that power."⁶

Beyond the knowledge of how to access the priesthood power they have been endowed with in the temple, women also gain in all the ordinances of the temple an even clearer knowledge of who they are and what they ultimately can become. The Lord has revealed that "the power of godliness," including the power to become like Him, is manifested through priesthood ordinances (Doctrine and Covenants 84:20). Thus, both women and men are able to ultimately become exalted beings like their Heavenly Parents. President Joseph Fielding Smith instructed, "Because of that priesthood and the *ordinances* thereof, every member of the Church, men and women alike, may know God."⁷ I do not believe we, as members of the Church, recognize the impact it has on us to literally know that we are children of Divine Parents and have the potential to be like Them. That knowledge gives us purpose, insight, perspective, power, and hope. Hopefully we all live our lives based on this foundational truth. In the temple, this truth becomes even more real, not only

> I do not believe we, as members of the Church, recognize the impact it has on us to literally know that we are children of Divine Parents and have the potential to be like Them. That knowledge gives us purpose, insight, perspective, power, and hope.

in the teachings of the ordinances but through the confirmation of the priesthood power of God.

Thus, both women and men leave the temple armed with priesthood power, having been clothed in the "garments of the holy priesthood." Elder Neil L. Andersen testified that as members of the Church "worthily participate in the ordinances of the priesthood, the Lord will give you greater strength, peace, and eternal perspective. Whatever your situation, your home will be 'blessed by the strength of priesthood power' and those close to you will more fully desire these blessings for themselves."[8]

What does this power received in the temple do for women? What kind of power do women have? Women who make and keep covenants in the temple have "the power of enlightenment, of testimony, and of understanding."[9] They can pray, receiving guidance from the Lord at an even greater level because of the endowment they have received in the temple. Women have the "power [to] thwart the forces of evil,"[10] or, in other words, to contend and win against the power of Satan in their own lives, in their homes, or while they travel. They have the "power . . . to use [their] gifts and capabilities with greater intelligence and increased effectiveness"[11] than they would have otherwise been able to. Women have the "power to overcome the sins of the world,"[12] are "better qualified to teach,"[13] and can protect and "strengthen their earthly families."[14]

These are still only a few of the powers promised and received in temple ordinances. Again, imagine how powerful this knowledge is for all covenant-keeping women. Imagine the strength this gives to our sister missionaries as they encounter confusion or evil forces, knowing that they have the power of God to teach with power, thwart evil forces, and have increased intellect. Imagine the strength this gives to a mother at home raising her children, knowing that this power of intelligence and teaching is real for her. Imagine the strength and security that could be felt by many women as they travel, speak, and teach to know that they are blessed with the power of the Lord as well as His authority to act and do His will. Imagine the difference this may make for a woman who is divorced or whose husband is inactive or away from the home for whatever reason, to know that she is endowed with these powers, that these powers exist in her home because she is there as a righteous, covenant-keeping daughter of God.

## PRIESTHOOD KEYS AND HOW THEY APPLY TO WOMEN INDIVIDUALLY AND IN THEIR FAMILIES

Just as there are different purposes behind priesthood keys in the hierarchical structure, keys have different uses in the patriarchal structure as well.

President Dallin H. Oaks taught that "one important difference between [the priesthood's] function in the Church and in the family is the fact that all priesthood authority *in the Church* functions under the direction of the one who holds the appropriate priesthood keys. In contrast, the authority that presides *in the family*—whether father or single-parent mother—functions in family matters without the need to get authorization from anyone holding priesthood keys."[15]

In the temple, presiding keys or keys of presidency of any kind are not given to men or women. Priesthood keys of presidency received in the hierarchical structure of the Church are necessary, however, for performing saving ordinances or for setting apart or for ordaining to priesthood offices, even within a family. Some of these saving ordinances, which are often performed by fathers for family members, include baptism, confirmation, sacrament, and ordination to priesthood offices. Although the covenant-keeping and ordained father holds the priesthood, he is not authorized to perform these ordinances without the permission of one who is ordained to a priesthood office. Thus, in some cases, the hierarchical and patriarchal priesthood overlap.[16]

## AUTHORITY AND POWER RECEIVED IN THE SEALING ORDINANCE

President Henry B. Eyring taught, "There is nothing that has come or will come into your family as important as the sealing blessings."[17] Because the great plan of happiness is dependent on families being sealed for eternity, it is impossible to talk of exaltation without discussing the topic of eternal marriage and the sealing ordinance. In so doing, I recognize the heartache many feel who have not yet had the opportunity to marry, who have a marriage that has not yet been solemnized in the temple, who have a spouse who is seemingly not living up to the covenants made in the temple, or who have had their eternal marriage broken through cancellation of the sealing. I am extremely sensitive to this topic because I myself have been married only three years and previously lived forty years being single, wondering if I would ever have the opportunity to marry in this life. I understand the pain that comes from being lonely, even with the comfort of the Holy Ghost. I have family members and dear friends who remain single, who have divorced, or who are currently married to spouses who are not living up to their temple covenants. That being said, I have no question that God will give us compensatory blessings, even if those blessings are delayed until the next life.

As difficult as it was for me to realize that being sealed to a spouse in the temple is part of the great plan of happiness, and that I didn't yet have it, it was still something I clung to, had a testimony of, and developed hope in. I recognized that the life I was living was in accordance with the Lord's will, and that at some point, whether in this life or the next, if I remained worthy, the Lord would bless me with the opportunity. I recognized and felt something was missing, similar to how I feel now with no children in our home, although I am happily married to my husband. The reality that some of us do not have ideal lives does not discredit the truth of eternal happiness. Frankly, none of us, whether married or single, will have the ideal life until we receive exaltation.

Although I am now sealed in the temple, I realize that making this covenant was merely the first step. Keeping the covenant is critical. President Russell M. Nelson taught: "The full realization of the blessings of a temple marriage is almost beyond our mortal comprehension. Such a marriage will continue to grow in the celestial realm. There we can become perfected. As Jesus ultimately received the fulness of the glory of the Father, so we may 'come unto the Father . . . and in due time receive of his fulness.'" He continued, "Celestial marriage is a pivotal part of preparation for eternal life. It requires one to be married to the right person, in the right place, by the right authority, and to obey that sacred covenant faithfully. Then one may be assured of exaltation in the celestial kingdom of God."[18]

I love the way President Nelson acknowledges that we are not yet perfect. None of us are. We do not marry perfection; in fact, there is no mortal perfection beyond that displayed by the Savior. I also love the truth that although we are not married to perfect people now, in the eternities we will not be married to anyone less. Our marriages will grow as we as couples put Christ in the center of all we do. As we grow closer to Christ, we cannot help but grow closer to each other in love, in character, in humor, in light, in glory, and in joy because it is Christ who, through His grace, makes it happen. We have entered into an order of the priesthood that allows Him to do so.

Elder Charles W. Penrose taught: "When a woman is sealed to a man holding the Priesthood, she becomes one with him. . . . The glory and power and dominion that he will exercise when he has the fulness of the Priesthood and becomes 'a king and a priest unto God,' she will share with him."[19] In the sealing ordinance, therefore, both husband and wife enter into the patriarchal order of the priesthood together, both receive authority together, and both receive power together, as this authority and this power are meant for and authorized to be used within the walls of their own eternal family home.

President Nelson taught, "To those couples who bear and share that priesthood worthily and remain faithful to the law of the everlasting covenant of eternal marriage, enduring the congested years and trials of diapers and dishes, crowded kitchen and thin pocketbook, service in the Church, education and the burning of the midnight oil, the Lord makes this promise: 'Ye shall come forth in the first resurrection; . . . and shall inherit thrones, kingdoms, principalities, and *powers,* dominions, . . . [and there] shall be a fulness and a continuation of the seeds forever and ever.'"[20]

Armed with priesthood power and authority, a sealed couple has started the process for her to become a queen and a priestess and for him to become a king and a priest, as equal partners, but with their own roles. As this topic of equal partnership and roles is confusing to many, let's look first at what the leaders of the Church have said recently about this topic of partnership.

## EQUAL PARTNERS

As explained earlier, in the hierarchical structure of the Church, the bishop presides over the ward, assisted by his counselors. Some have erroneously suggested that, similarly, the husband alone presides in the home, while the wife is like his counselor. Elder L. Tom Perry reminded the brethren that in their role as the leader in the family, their wife is their companion. Quoting President Gordon B. Hinckley, he then taught: "In this Church the man neither walks ahead of his wife nor behind his wife but at her side. They are coequals." Elder Perry explained, "Since the beginning, God has instructed mankind that marriage should unite husband and wife together in unity." He then adamantly stated: "Therefore, there is not a president or a vice president in a family. The couple works together eternally for the good of the family. They are united together in word, in deed, and in action as they lead, guide, and direct their family unit. They are on equal footing. They plan and organize the affairs of the family jointly and unanimously as they move forward."[21]

The family proclamation is clear on this beautiful explanation of the wife-and-husband partnership role: "In these sacred responsibilities, fathers and mothers are obligated to help one another as equal partners."[22] On the roles of husbands and wives working together as equal partners, President Nelson instructed, "There is a division of labor in

> Over the years, I have had many opportunities to watch married couples. . . . It seems that in the relationships that thrived, there was no competition between the husband and wife. Neither was "in charge" of the other—neither "wore the pants" in the relationship—but each recognized the importance of each of their divine roles and of loving and serving and being selfless together.

marriage. The husband is an external force. His normal duty is to provide and protect. The wife is an internal force. Her normal duty is to care, nurture, and to teach. Neither husband nor wife is 'the boss.'"[23]

Over the years, I have had many opportunities to watch married couples. At times, it has felt like I have had a front-row seat at the marriages of my siblings, close friends, nephews and nieces, extended family members, missionary couples, and those in Church leadership. It seems that in the relationships that thrived, there was no competition between the husband and wife. Neither was "in charge" of the other—neither "wore the pants" in the relationship—but each recognized the importance of each of their divine roles and of loving and serving and being selfless together.

The phrase *equal partners* seems to mean what it says. It doesn't mean one rules over the other. In fact, many, quoting the Bible, teach that a man is to rule over his wife. President Gordon B. Hinckley took critical issue with this notion when he declared:

> Some men who are evidently unable to gain respect by the goodness of their lives, use as justification for their actions the statement that Eve was told that Adam should rule over her. How much sadness, how much tragedy, how much heartbreak has been caused through centuries of time by weak men who have used that as a scriptural warrant for atrocious behavior! They do not recognize that the same account indicates that Eve was given as a helpmeet to Adam. The facts are that they stood, side by side, in the garden. They were expelled from the garden together, and they worked together side by side in gaining their bread by the sweat of their brows.[24]

The leaders of the Church are absolutely adamant about the importance of women and men, especially husband and wives, working together as partners. Both wife and husband alike need to understand the scripture revealed to Joseph Smith regarding the priesthood that "no power or influence can or ought to be maintained by virtue of the priesthood, only by persuasion, by long-suffering, by gentleness and meekness, and by love unfeigned; by kindness, and pure knowledge" (Doctrine and Covenants 121:41–42).

## PRIESTHOOD POWER IS LOST WHEN THERE IS UNRIGHTEOUSNESS IN THE FAMILY

A short while ago, I had a female student in my office who explained that taking the Eternal Family class was hard for her, especially when we talked about relationships between husband and wife. With tears streaming down her cheeks, she expressed that she was afraid of marriage, and although she was happy for those who have great marriages, the risk of marriage was too high for her. She went on to describe the relationship her parents had, including her father's continued use of the phrase, "I hold the priesthood, so you need to listen and obey," when conflict between her parents arose. She wondered how it was possible that her father in such an angry state could have "priesthood power" over her mom just because he held the priesthood.

Among other things, I explained to this student that her father, in those moments, likely was not worthy of the priesthood power he declared he possessed. I shared with her, as I have with many other students over the years, the following quote from President Gordon B. Hinckley to the women of the Church: "Unfortunately a few of you may be married to men who are abusive. Some of them put on a fine face before the world during the day and come home in the evening, set aside their self-discipline, and on the slightest provocation fly into outbursts of anger. No man who engages in such evil and unbecoming behavior is worthy of the priesthood of God. No man who so conducts himself is worthy of the privileges of the house of the Lord."[25]

One of the major abuses of this power is when men who hold the priesthood declare to their wives, "I hold the priesthood, therefore I have the final say." Or, "I appreciate your opinion, but since I hold the priesthood, you've got to do what I say." Recently, one of my students explained that her mother was never allowed to pray in the family or participate in family scripture study because her father "held the priesthood and believed it wasn't good for the family to have the wife so spiritually involved." The daughter hadn't heard her mother pray in years! President

Spencer W. Kimball declared that such a man "should not be honored in his priesthood."[26] I would add that the same is true for women. Although these stories may seem extreme, it may be worth taking an inventory on how the priesthood is used and discussed within our families.

## Couples' Responsibilities to Each Other

President Russell M. Nelson reminds each man that "his highest and most important priesthood duty is to honor and sustain his wife." The same is true of women supporting their husbands. President Nelson continues: "An enduring marriage results when both husband and wife regard their union as one of the two most important commitments they will ever make. The other commitment of everlasting consequence is to the Lord."[27]

One of the most beautiful examples I saw of this covenant relationship between husband and wife was during the final years of my mother's life. The love, protection, and trust between my father and mother became extremely apparent. During her final months and weeks as she was dying of brain cancer, her ability to reason began to fail. I had been accustomed to giving her medicine on a regular basis, and, as some of my siblings came in to help during the final weeks, they did so as well. Right before she passed away, my mother began to think that we, her children, were administering poison rather than medicine to her. I can't begin to explain how painful it was to have her say to me, "Barbara, why are you trying to kill me with that poison?" I would explain to her that I wasn't—that I was doing what she had previously asked me to do and what the doctors had prescribed. There came a point when she no longer would even believe me. At the very end of her life, every time I tried to give her the medicine, she would reply, "I need to speak with my husband before I take this." I would get my dad, who would kneel by her side, take both her hands in his, and, looking right into her eyes, would say, "Sharon, I know it's hard, but you need to take this medicine."

My mother would simply respond, "Al, I believe this medicine is killing me, but if you believe it is the right thing to do, I'll do it." He would respond in the affirmative, put the pills on her tongue, and place the straw gently in her mouth, and she would suck and swallow.

For much of my mother's life, she stayed at home while my father worked and held many callings. I saw them as equals. During my father's later years, as he struggled with major clinical depression, I saw her open the windows to bring in light, study the scriptures, sing happy tunes, fast and pray, and support him and the family, even as he continued to work and hold important Church callings. They were a team. They were in love. I love them for it and am so grateful for their incredible example. I remember when my dad would go on business trips, my mom would call on family members to pray. We missed having Dad in the home, at times for weeks, but we knew that we were safe and protected and well taken care of by Mom. We knew that we could never pit Mom against Dad or vice versa. In fact, I don't know that there was much worse we could do than to go to one or the other of our parents when one had already given an answer. They were on the same page. Sure, they disagreed sometimes—they both had strong opinions, and each had a life full of experiences—but when a decision was made, they made it together.

President James E. Faust taught that "every father is to his family a patriarch and every mother a matriarch as coequals in their distinctive parental roles."[28] Again, when we enter into the patriarchal order, we enter into a family order of government in which leadership is horizontal, not vertical. Both husband and wife recognize and utilize the gifts and talents of each other and love each other for the betterment of the entire family system. President M. Russell Ballard, instructing Church members on the family proclamation, clarified: "As the proclamation clearly states, men and women, though spiritually equal, are entrusted with different but equally significant roles. These roles complement each other. Men are given stewardship over the sacred ordinances of the priesthood. To women, God gives stewardship over bestowing and nurturing mortal life, including providing physical bodies for God's spirit children and guiding those children toward a knowledge of gospel truths. These stewardships, equally sacred and important, do not involve any false ideas about domination or subordination. Each stewardship is essential for the spiritual progression of all family members, parents and children alike."[29]

When it comes to stewardship for the couple and family, President Ballard explains that this must be "understood in terms of obligations and responsibilities—and in terms of love, service, and interdependence." He then clarifies that "men who attempt to dominate their wives, who seek to exercise unrighteous dominion without regard to spousal counsel and sensitivities, simply don't understand that such actions are contrary to God's will."[30]

## Fathers Preside in the Family and Are the Patriarchs

Much has been said recently by leaders of the Church on what it means for a father to preside in his family. President M. Russell Ballard, going point by point through the family proclamation, spoke clearly on what presiding means for the father. He instructed that the father's role is to perform priesthood ordinances, give priesthood blessings, and pray for and with family members. "They set an example of respect and love for their eternal companion and mother of their children. In all things they follow the example of the Savior and strive to be worthy of His name and His blessing. Fathers should seek constantly for guidance from the Holy Ghost so they will know what to do, what to say, and also know what *not* to do and what *not* to say. They serve the family and the Church in the spirit of love and enthusiasm."[31]

This presiding, the Lord's type of presiding, is done in love and righteousness. It entails serving selflessly, lifting others, working hard, and following the guidance of the Holy Ghost. It is critically different from the world's definition of *presiding*.

Similarly, Elder Dale G. and Sister Ruth L. Renlund teach that presiding in the home for a priesthood holder means that he "serves in accordance with the doctrine of the priesthood." They continue, "His life will be 'founded on the teachings of the Lord Jesus Christ,' and he will, with his wife as an equal partner, establish a home built on 'principles of faith, prayer, repentance, forgiveness, respect, love, compassion, work, and wholesome recreational activity.'" This presiding priesthood holder, they explain, will "acknowledge error and seek forgiveness; he will be quick to offer praise; he will be considerate of family members' preferences; he will feel the great weight of responsibility to provide the 'necessities of life and protection' for his family; he will treat his wife with the utmost respect and deference. He will listen to understand the challenges facing each family member and then go about helping in the manner the Savior would. He will bless his family."³²

President Nelson has taught: "Ideally, the Latter-day Saint family is presided over by a worthy man who holds the priesthood. . . . He who is the Father of us all and the source of this authority demands that governance in the home be in love and righteousness." Note how President Nelson describes what he hopes presiding fathers will do in the home:

> You fathers can help with the dishes, care for a crying baby, and change a diaper. And perhaps some Sunday you could get the children ready for Church, and your wife could sit in the car and honk.
>
> "Husbands, love your wives, even as Christ also loved the church, and gave himself for it." With that kind of love, brethren, we will be better husbands and fathers, more loving and spiritual leaders. Happiness at home is most likely to be achieved when practices there are founded upon the teachings of Jesus Christ. Ours is the responsibility to ensure that we have family prayer, scripture study, and family home evening. Ours is the responsibility to prepare our children to receive the ordinances of salvation and exaltation and the blessings promised to tithe payers. Ours is the privilege to bestow priesthood blessings of healing, comfort, and direction.³³

In teaching what it means to preside, I often help students focus on what the Brethren do not mention. President Nelson, for example, does not mention making the final decision, bossing, or even being in charge, but rather talks of love, service, help, and ensuring sacred family time. It is clear that presiding requires being like and treating others as Christ would.

If there is an emphasis in the prophets' teachings to the men who are presiding in their homes, it is to work harder to care for their relationships with their wives and children. President Nelson explained to men that "the best thing you can do for your children is to love and care for their mother. Let that love show. Let your children and grandchildren grow in the comfort and confidence of a cherished mother. Help her to achieve the full measure of her creation."[34]

I remember as a teenager walking into the kitchen after a volleyball practice at the high school. My mother was standing in front of the sink, water and soapsuds splashed onto her stomach, as was quite common. In response to her asking how my day went, I let her know in an unkind tone and manner how my day had been great until she had forgotten to pick me up at the high school and I'd had to walk home. I don't remember much of the conversation, but I must have been loud enough and hurtful enough for my father to not only hear but correct me. I had no idea he was home, as it was late in the afternoon. As he walked into the kitchen, I could see the pain in his eyes. He walked right between me and my mom, put his pointer finger in my face, looked me directly in the eyes, and in a firm yet tempered tone declared, "That is my wife!" I can honestly say, in my entire life up to that point, that was as forceful as my dad had ever been with me. I quickly ran downstairs, embarrassed and ashamed. It wasn't long, however, before my dad knocked on my door, entered the room, put his arm around me, and explained to me that because he loved me and my mother so much, he would not allow my mother to be treated that way, especially by his daughter. My mother was his priority, his queen! I loved him for it then, and I look forward to the time when he will be with her again.

On one of our family trek trips to Wyoming, I remember stopping at Rock Creek Hollow. Although at that age I was unfamiliar with much of the history, I remember reading the names and ages and hearing the stories of those who were rescued, those who did the rescuing, and those who passed away in that holy place. I was impressed that almost all who passed away were male. I remember thinking that strange, as it seemed that the children and the women, those who perhaps were not as physically strong, would have been the ones to pass away first. I brought that question to my mother, who simply replied, "I would imagine that many of those men and boys were like your father and brothers, willing to give literally anything for their wife and siblings." I felt that her explanation was correct.

Elder Jeffrey R. Holland was recently asked by a young father what it meant to preside in the home. Elder Holland responded, "When the

Savior washed the feet of the Twelve, He was teaching that great lesson of stewardship and leadership and love.... If you could attain that spirit, I would never, ever worry about you being a husband and a father, if you were that devoted to your wife and that devoted to your children that they meant everything that they could and should mean to you, and in that deferential way you would wash their feet and change the baby's diapers and take time with your wife to listen to Beethoven together."[35]

In teaching the important role of the family, President Nelson often asks men about their various priesthood responsibilities. He has stated that many "mention their important Church duties to which they have been called. Too few remember their responsibilities at home. Yet priesthood offices, keys, callings, and quorums are meant to exalt families. Priesthood authority has been restored so that families can be sealed eternally. So brethren, your foremost priesthood duty is to nurture your marriage—to care for, respect, honor, and love your wife. Be a blessing to her and your children."[36] In other words, if men preside correctly in their families, their families will come first and Church callings second. In setting those priorities, men are actually putting God first, then their wives and children, followed by their Church callings. A correct understanding and application of priesthood responsibilities for men will naturally lead to an improved home-centered and Church-supported organization.

> In the home, parents are coequals. If a father or husband is not in the home, by simple default, the mother, wife, or single sister presides. As a single sister, I so appreciated and respected my home teachers, who would ask at the beginning and end of their visits whom I would like to have pray.

## Mothers Presiding in the Home

As President Dallin H. Oaks said, when his father passed away, he thought he would be presiding as a twelve-year-old priesthood holder in the family. He stated that he was shocked to learn that his mother was actually presiding and realized that there was something he did not understand regarding the priesthood in the home. This confusion for Elder Oaks is alive and well today. In the home, parents are coequals. If a father or husband is not in the home, by simple default, the mother, wife, or single sister presides. As a single sister, I so appreciated and respected my home teachers, who would ask at the beginning and end of their visits whom I would like to have pray. Even my father, when he would come to my home for a family event, would remind me that it was *my* home and thus my responsibility to lead out. Any man, of whatever position, who acts in a position of authority when entering someone's home other than his own is out of place. Any man who does so to a woman, regardless of marital status, although often unintentionally, is demeaning to her and her sacred role.

## Motherhood and Nurturing

In regard to women's role in God's great eternal plan, President Nelson reminds us that "priesthood is the power of God. Its ordinances and covenants are to bless men and women alike. By that power, the earth was created. Under the direction of the Father, Jehovah was the creator. As Michael, Adam did his part. He became the first man. But, in spite of the power and glory of creation to that point, the final link in the chain of creation was still missing. All the purposes of the world and all that was in the world would be brought to naught without woman—a keystone in the priesthood arch of creation."[37] What is the purpose of the keystone in an arch? Webster's dictionary defines the keystone as the wedge-shaped piece at the crown of an arch that locks the other pieces in place, or something on which associated things depend for support. Often, we speak of the Book of Mormon as the keystone of the gospel; without it, the gospel would fall. In a similar vein, President Nelson is teaching that woman is critical to the priesthood; without women, the purpose of creation would be meaningless.

Helping clarify the priesthood role of women in our Heavenly Father's plan, Sister Julie B. Beck, former Relief Society General President, stated: "The priesthood role of fathers is to preside and pass priesthood ordinances to the next generation. The priesthood role of mothers is to influence. These are essential, complementary, and interdependent responsibilities."[38] In another setting, Sister Beck taught that "the priesthood duty of sisters is to create life, to nurture it, to prepare it for covenants of the Lord."[39] In fact, as John A. Widtsoe carefully proclaimed, "Motherhood is an eternal part of Priesthood."[40]

Over the years, many Church leaders have taken great care to assure all women that, regardless of their marital status or ability to provide bodies for children, they are mothers, and by divine right, all mothers have been given the responsibility to nurture. President Nelson clarified that "anytime I use the word *mother*, I am not talking only about women who have given birth or adopted children in this life. I am speaking about *all* of our Heavenly Parents' adult daughters. *Every* woman is a mother by virtue of her eternal divine destiny."[41]

For some women, the term *nurture* feels demeaning. It has almost the exact opposite connotation from the word *preside*. According to the Lord, however, motherhood, and thus nurturing, is divine. In fact, President Hugh B. Brown taught that "Jesus honored womanhood when he came to this earth as a little child through the sacred and glorious agency of motherhood; thus motherhood became akin to Godhood."[42] The First Presidency called motherhood "the highest, holiest service . . . assumed by mankind."[43]

As a single woman for years, and now a married woman with no children, I find this truth most comforting. Although I do work full time, I feel blessed that the Lord has trusted me with the teaching of His children. Among my greatest joys in life is spending time "nurturing": teaching, playing with, reading to, supporting, and loving my nephews and nieces—they are among my greatest joys. I appreciate so much my siblings and in-laws who have allowed me to be a part of nurturing their children. I pray for them, think of them, fast for them, laugh with them, cry for them, and have the highest hopes for them. I've appreciated the callings I have been blessed to have in Primary, Young Women, and Relief

Society, and I often try to teach and nurture as if those I have been called to nurture were mine. I absolutely have loved teaching the youth in seminary and now the young adults as a religious educator at BYU. Of course, I would love to have children of my own, but the blessing of being able to nurture in my family, callings, and profession is among the greatest the Lord has given me. I have no doubt that one day, in mortality or in the next life, the Lord will bless me and my husband with a multitude of children. In the meantime, nurturing those in my own family and those I teach is among my greatest priorities. Recently, President Nelson praised women who "know how to call upon the powers of heaven to protect and strengthen their husbands, their children, and others they love."[44] Nurturing is more than loving and caring, feeding and changing; nurturing is teaching, and especially teaching the gospel.

It is in nurturing that the keys and power of the endowment regarding knowledge and truth are most poignantly combined with the divine mandate to mother. Covenant-keeping members are specially endowed and promised mysteries and knowledge from God. What better place to use these gifts than in the family? To the women of the Church, President Henry B. Eyring declared: "Part of the Lord's current sharing of knowledge relates to accelerating His pouring out eternal truth on the heads and into the hearts of His people. He has made clear that the daughters of Heavenly Father will play a primary role in that miraculous acceleration. One evidence of the miracle is His leading His living prophet to put far greater emphasis on gospel instruction in the home and within the family." He then explains how faithful sisters will be a primary force in helping the Lord pour out knowledge on the Saints. "In the proclamation, He gave sisters charge to be the principal gospel educators in the family in these words: 'Mothers are primarily responsible for the nurture of their children.' This includes the nurture of gospel truth and knowledge."[45]

Nurturing, therefore, for women means that they are to be the "principal gospel educators." Put this in context of the two-hour church block, the lowering of age for the sister missionaries, the invitation for girls starting at age eight to attend the general women's session, the training of our Primary girls to enter the temple, and the increased responsibility of our young women in vicarious work for the dead. Consider the prophet's invitation to all women, young and older, to spend more time in the temple, study the Book of Mormon, and use their time more wisely. It is clear that women are taking on an enhanced role both in the family-centered, Church-supported organizational structure and in the gathering of Israel.

The role of the mother in a home and in society cannot be overemphasized. I believe that for many women and men, our problem isn't in what we see, as President Eyring has taught, but in what we cannot see.[46] So many worldly things are noticed because awards are given, accolades are shown, speeches are visible, books are buyable, performances are watched, money is made, and raises are given. Most worldly reinforcement is visible, seemingly valued, verifiable, and often immediate. Mothering, by contrast, is often quiet, individual, gentle, frequently anonymous, selfless, and with no accolades. It is in the later years, and especially in the eternities, when we will come to understand the full worth of mothers. The leaders of the Church, and especially the Lord, already know.

## ETERNAL FAMILY IS OUR PROPHETIC PRIORITY

In today's world, it is so easy to get trapped in a society that is telling women what is most important and forgetting God. It is so easy and enticing to believe that something, anything, is more important than the home. The irony of the situation is that if families, as they are ordained of God, fail, society will fail, economies will fail, and governments will fail.

President Joseph F. Smith taught: "Men and women often seek to substitute some other life for that of the home; they would make themselves believe that the home means restraint; that the highest liberty is the fullest opportunity to move about at will. There is no happiness without service, and there is no service greater than that which converts the home into a divine institution, and which promotes and preserves family life."[47]

I believe it is important to make it clear that making family a priority doesn't have to wait until one is married or has children. I remember being at a meeting one day in which all of us were asked to stand and talk about our families. A single sister sitting across the room stood, introduced herself, and then simply stated, "I don't have a family, so I guess that's it." I knew her enough to know that she did have a family. She had parents, siblings, nephews and nieces, cousins, and more. I felt sorry for her in that moment, as I do not believe she realized what a great priority and blessing these family members are. I know that in my own professional life, I have received criticism for acknowledging by number how many nephews and nieces my husband and I have. Frankly, if I had the space, I would include all of their names and what I love about them as well.

Although the world may be confused about the importance of home, family, partnership, and equality between husband and wife, and the priority of family in God's great plan, the prophets and leaders of this Church are not. The more the family comes under attack, the more the world strives to change definitions and confuse gender roles, the more the Lord through His prophets and leaders has and likely will continue to send a clear message regarding the family.

# Chapter 6

# THAT WE MIGHT BE ONE

Prior to His crucifixion, the Savior prayed for His disciples, "That they all may be one; as thou, Father, art in me, and I in thee, that they also may be one in us" (John 17:21). Even during the Creation, God commanded, "Therefore shall a man leave his father and his mother, and shall cleave unto his wife: and they shall be one flesh" (Genesis 2:24). After King Benjamin delivered his sermon on the Atonement of Jesus Christ, the people "all cried with one voice" and recognized "that because of the Spirit of the Lord Omnipotent" a "mighty change" had been wrought in them. As a result, King Benjamin gave all who had "entered into the covenant with God" a new name, even "the name of Christ" (Mosiah 5:1–9). During the early days of the Restoration, the Lord Himself declared, "If ye are not one ye are not mine" (Doctrine and Covenants 38:27). President Henry B. Eyring said: "Our Heavenly Father wants our hearts to be knit together. That union in love is not simply an ideal. It is a necessity."[1]

When the Saints were called to settle Jackson County, Missouri, it seems that the Lord was trying to help them to simultaneously prepare for their temple covenants, take advantage of their priesthood privileges, create Zion, gather scattered Israel, and prepare the world for the Second Coming. A large feat for sure! In sections 50 through 58 of the Doctrine and Covenants, the Lord, through the Prophet Joseph Smith, explains the things that both build and destroy Zion. In summary, it seems that the overall principle that creates Zion is unity.

This truth has not changed today. In order for both men and women to understand their priesthood privileges, in order for us to create the family-centered, Church-supported organization the Lord is emphasizing through His apostles and prophet, in order to gather Israel and prepare the world for the Second Coming of the Savior, covenant women must be unified with those of other cultures and situations, with each other as women, with the youth, with men at Church, within the family, and especially with the Lord.

## UNITY AMONG ALL PEOPLE OF FAITH

Bishop Gérald Caussé taught: "In this Church there are no strangers and no outcasts. There are only brothers and sisters. The knowledge that we have of an Eternal Father helps us be more sensitive to the brotherhood and sisterhood that should exist among all men and women upon the earth."[2] As I have been involved extensively in interfaith work as a chaplain for higher education and in my current position at BYU on the interfaith council, I have come to appreciate people of other faiths as never before. I have learned to appreciate the Sabbath day from the teachings and example of my Jewish friends. I love and understand Emma Smith with a perspective I could never have gained except from members of the Community of Christ. I've learned patience from humanists, acceptance from Unitarians, true friendship and peacemaking from the Quakers, and on and on. As members of The Church of Jesus Christ of Latter-day Saints, we do not have a monopoly on truth or on goodness. Some have asked if my relationships with those of other faiths undermine or compromise my testimony. Absolutely not! The more I understand those of other faiths, the more grateful I am, not only for them but for the truth that has been bestowed on us as covenant keepers.

## UNITY BETWEEN WOMEN

My students often lament that the prophets are always much harder on the men than the women. I'm quick to respond that the leaders of the Church have been warning the women and speaking to them as well, just in a different way. Who can forget, for example, the story President Monson told of the woman complaining about her neighbor's dirty laundry only to find out that it was the judgmental woman's windows, not the neighbor's laundry, that needed the cleaning. President Monson declared:

> My dear sisters, each of you is unique. You are different from each other in many ways. There are those of you who are married. Some of you stay at home with your children, while others of you work outside your homes. Some of you are empty nesters. There are those of you who are married but do not have children. There are those who are divorced, those who are widowed. Many of you are single women. Some of you have college degrees; some of you do not. There are those who can afford the latest fashions and those who are lucky to have one appropriate Sunday outfit. Such differences are almost endless. Do these differences tempt us to judge one another?

He then continued with a quote, which he called a "profound truth," from Mother Teresa, "If you judge people, you have no time to love them."[3] After quoting the Savior's admonition that we "love one another, as I have loved you," President Monson asked, *"can we love one another, as the Savior has commanded, if we judge each other?"* He answered, "No, we cannot."[4]

This warning and concern over women being judgmental or self-righteous is not new. The Prophet Joseph Smith addressed the Relief Society on this topic several times. As he prepared the women to enter the temple and take their rightful places in their families and society, he spoke on how they treated each other. For example, he counseled the women to "not injure the character of any one,"[5] and even asked the society to "hold your tongues about things of no moment," as "a little tale will set the world on fire."[6] It was to these early Relief Society women that Joseph taught, "Nothing is so much calculated to lead people to forsake sin as to take them by the hand and watch over them with tenderness."[7] He also called the women to repentance when he declared, "We are full of selfishness—the devil flatters us that we are very righteous, while we are feeding on the faults of others." He continued, "If the sisters love the Lord let them feed the sheep and not destroy them."[8]

As a child and youth, I looked forward with excitement to Mother's Day. As crazy as it sounds, I loved the thrill of watching my mom, year after year, get the prize for having the most children. To me, that was the ultimate sign of success for a woman, and from my perspective, no other woman compared to my mom. I remember my mom, however, always being a little embarrassed about the prize, stating that it was inappropriate, insensitive, and given in poor judgment. Although she was always gracious in the moment, I remember my mom explaining to us that success wasn't in the number of children one had, any more than it was in the amount of money one earned or the rewards of the world. Success was in following the Spirit. Oh, how grateful I have become for my mother's wise tutoring!

I would add that success is also not in whether our marriages have survived or what academic degrees we have achieved. Success is not measured by the jobs our spouses have or the promotions we have received in our own jobs. Success is not in where we live, what callings we receive, or what kind of clothes we wear. Success isn't in how long we live, how healthy we are, or how our children turn out. Success is in following the Spirit. Sister Julie B. Beck declared, "The ability to qualify for, receive, and act on personal revelation is the single most important skill that can be acquired in this life."[9] Regarding this quote, President M. Russell Ballard simply said, "I agree with her."[10]

> I believe that one of the keys to not judging or being self-righteous is in the simple recognition that the Spirit guides each person on a different path.

I believe that one of the keys to not judging or being self-righteous is in the simple recognition that the Spirit guides each person on a different path. Among my own sisters, sisters-in-law, aunts, and cousins, there are those who were married at age eighteen, and then there's me, who married at forty. There are those who work full time and those who stay home with their children. There are those who have college degrees and those who do not. There are some who have divorced, some who have inactive children, and some whose children have passed away or left the Church altogether. I have sisters of various nationalities and backgrounds. Among my students and members in my ward and stake, there are those who have same-gender attraction, some who have lost jobs, others who have struggled through adultery, pornography addictions, deaths of loved ones, and a host of other challenges. As the Church continues to expand, there will be many more women with many more differences.

President James E. Faust taught: "Everywhere there can be a 'unity of the faith.' Each group [or person] brings special gifts and talents to the table of the Lord. We can all learn much of value from each other. But each of us should also voluntarily seek to enjoy all of the unifying and saving covenants, ordinances, and doctrines of the gospel of the Lord Jesus Christ. . . . Our real strength is not so much in our diversity but in our spiritual and doctrinal unity."[11]

We as covenant-keeping women must be each other's best cheerleaders, forgiving quickly, assuming the best, building up, teaching truth, letting things go, and growing in charity. Sister Bonnie L. Oscarson, former Young Women General President, stated: "We are unified in building the kingdom of God and in the covenants which we have made, no matter what our circumstances. . . . If there are barriers, it is because we ourselves have created them. We must stop concentrating on our differences and look for what we have in common; then we can begin to realize our greatest potential and achieve the greatest good in this world."[12]

I am grateful for the many female friends and role models the Lord has placed in my life. I'm so grateful for those who helped me as a young adult to make decisions based not on culture or on what they did, but rather on what the Lord was trying to teach me. I remember one instance, after I had graduated from BYU and was working on my doctoral degree, when I was sitting in the car with my bishop's wife, who had become a dear friend. She was married, had three beautiful children, and lived in many regards a very different life than I did. I don't remember the specifics of our conversation, but I remember how much I trusted and appreciated her. When I doubted myself, she set me back on my feet and helped me to see that the impressions I was feeling to teach religion at BYU were more than just passing thoughts, but inspiration. More than that, she expressed complete confidence in my ability to do it.

I have thought of how different my future could have been if she had judged me for planning on working full time rather than getting married. How would I have felt if my mother, while I was growing up, had caused me to believe that my life wouldn't be successful unless I too received awards for the number of children I had borne. Many women struggle enough when they are exceptions rather than the rule; although it is important to teach the rule, it is critical that we are kind, generous, and thoughtful to the exceptions. All of us will be an exception at some point in our lives. The hymn "As Sisters in Zion" summarizes much of this sentiment:

> *As sisters in Zion, we'll all work together;*
> *The blessings of God on our labors we'll seek.*
> *We'll build up his kingdom with earnest endeavor;*
> *We'll comfort the weary and strengthen the weak.*
>
> *The errand of angels is given to women;*
> *And this is a gift that, as sisters, we claim:*
> *To do whatsoever is gentle and human,*
> *To cheer and to bless in humanity's name.*
>
> *How vast is our purpose, how broad is our mission,*
> *If we but fulfill it in spirit and deed.*
> *Oh, naught but the Spirit's divinest tuition*
> *Can give us the wisdom to truly succeed.*[13]

Although I may not be perfect in recognizing the Spirit, I can confidently say that the Spirit has never caused me to feel contentious, never inspired me to judge unrighteously, gossip, hold a grudge, or be offended. He has inspired me to forgive quickly, bear another's burden, search my soul and repent, speak kindly, and be more compassionate. In every way, I believe the Spirit is asking me to have more charity. President Thomas S. Monson described charity this way: "Charity is having patience with someone who has let us down. It is resisting the impulse to become offended easily. It is accepting weaknesses and shortcomings. It is accepting people as they truly are. It is looking beyond physical appearances to attributes that will not dim through time. It is resisting the impulse to categorize others."

He then gives examples of what charity looks like today: "Charity, that pure love of Christ, is manifest when a group of young women from a singles ward travels hundreds of miles to attend the funeral services for the mother of one of their Relief Society sisters. Charity is shown when devoted visiting teachers return month after month, year after year to the same uninterested, somewhat critical sister. It is evident when an elderly widow is remembered and taken to ward functions and to Relief Society activities. It is felt when the sister sitting alone in Relief Society receives the invitation, 'Come—sit by us.'"[14] As covenant-keeping women, we are commissioned to save souls and to be a part of the gathering of Israel. I believe that the only way we can do that is if we "cherish one another, watch over one another, comfort one another," with the intent of one day sitting "down in heaven together."[15]

## UNITY WITH YOUNG WOMEN

For years I have gone on pioneer treks with family, work, young adult wards, youth groups, and friends. One of my favorite and most memorable experiences on the trek is almost always the "women's pull," in which the women, young and old, pull the handcarts up a steep slope by themselves while the men, young and old, look on. One particular women's pull stands out in my mind. It was during the hottest part of a hot Wyoming day. While the young women were being pumped up to fulfill the task ahead of them, the young men were being instructed not to help any of the young women, no matter how difficult it became for them. As the young women began to pull their carts up the steep slope, I was thrilled to see how well they were doing. One handcart after another went up the hill with the young women singing as they pulled and pushed in their pioneer costumes. I proudly watched as the young women who had made it to the top of the hill came running down to help the struggling young women at the bottom. It didn't take long, however, to recognize that even with all the energy, stamina, and optimism these young women had, they were becoming tired, dehydrated, and weak.

Wanting to allow the young women to have their moment, but also realizing that as women we need to help each other, I started running (wobbling) down the hill to help. I got only a few feet, however, before one of the Relief Society sisters caught my apron, held me back, and said, "The young women need to learn to do it by themselves." Out of respect for her, but against my better judgment, I stood back and held my tongue. At this moment, I had never been prouder of the young men who "broke the rules." Many of the priests got out of line and started pulling and pushing the wagons alongside the young women. They could not help themselves. In no way was there a demeaning or degrading attitude shown; rather, a feeling of love, appreciation, and joy enveloped the youth.

Although I am grateful for those young men, the idea of "the young women need to learn to do it by themselves" still haunts me. As sisters in the Relief Society, I believe we should be running to the aid of those young women, ever watchful to give a hand as well as to accept their help. We all need each other. In this world of confusion, why would we stand back and watch them struggle? There is a difference between doing it for them (creating a sense of entitlement) and walking beside them, helping them, lifting them when they fall. I'm grateful that in this case we had worthy young men to help, but if they weren't there, ready to step in, who would have stepped in instead, in our place as mothers, aunts and leaders? It was a "women's pull."

I spoke to a young adult woman who recently left the Church. She explained the struggle of having lost her child to a miscarriage while her husband was away. Not knowing whom to call for help, she Googled, "how to find faith as a Mormon woman?" Antagonistic material consumed her for the next six weeks as she "figured it out by herself," not wanting to "bother or take the time of" the women in her life who were busy with their own lives. If we aren't there as covenant women, in the path, on the side, in front, pulling, pushing, and walking beside our sisters, I'm confident that someone else or something else will be doing the work we should have been doing.

Sister Bonnie L. Oscarson addressed this concern as well in her April 2018 general conference talk. Quoting *Handbook 2,* she instructed the worldwide audience that "the work of salvation within our wards includes 'member missionary work, convert retention, activation of less-active members, temple and family history work, and teaching the gospel.'"[16] She continued: "This work is directed by our faithful bishops, who hold priesthood keys for their ward. For many years now, our presidency has been asking the question 'Which of these areas mentioned should our young women *not* be involved in?' The answer is that they have something to contribute in *all* areas of this work."

> If we aren't there as covenant women, in the path, on the side, in front, pulling, pushing, and walking beside our sisters, I'm confident that someone else or something else will be doing the work we should have been doing.

Sister Oscarson then asked members of ward councils to use the young women as resources to help the needs of the ward. She said: "Just as our Aaronic Priesthood holders have been invited to labor with their fathers and other men of the Melchizedek Priesthood, our young women can be called upon to provide service and minister to the needs of ward members with their mothers or other exemplary sisters. They are capable, eager, and willing to do so much more than merely attend church on Sundays!" Sister Oscarson then added an insightful reason for the importance of using these young women: "As we consider the roles that our young women will be expected to assume in the near future, we might ask ourselves what kind of experiences we could provide for them now that will help with their preparation to be missionaries, gospel scholars, leaders in the Church auxiliaries, temple workers, wives, mothers, mentors, examples, and friends. They can actually begin now to fill many of those roles."[17]

In recent years young women have a more significant role in the temple, serve missions at an earlier age, attend the general women's session at age eight, prepare at an earlier age to enter the temple both to perform baptisms and receive their endowments, have more agency in planning Young Women activities, including Young Women camp, and become ministering partners for other women in the ward starting at age thirteen.

Because so often bishops feel that their primary responsibility is the young men—perhaps because the bishop is president of the priests quorum, among other things—there may be a tendency to overlook the young women. Sister Oscarson reminded bishops: "Just as one of your highest priorities is to preside over the Aaronic Priesthood quorums, *Handbook 2* explains that 'the bishop and his counselors provide priesthood leadership for the Young Women organization. They watch over and strengthen individual young women, working closely with parents and Young Women leaders in this effort.'"[18]

With so much being required of these young women in the future, it is critical that they receive the proper teaching, training, attention, mentoring, experiences, and more while they are young. That being said, we as adult women must recognize how much we need these young women as well. I cannot begin to express the gratitude I have and the blessings that have been poured upon me due to my relationships with the young women of this Church. They have taught me by their examples, love, openness, kindness, acceptance, brilliance, and testimonies. From one who has worked professionally for years with the young women and young adult women, as well as in callings and in my own family, I'm confident that the Church and especially our families and the world are in good hands. The Lord has saved this generation of young women for a reason. We need each other!

## UNITY BETWEEN MEN AND WOMEN AT CHURCH

Elder John A Widtsoe wisely instructed, "The Priesthood when exercised righteously unites men and women; it never separates them, unless either group, by their own acts, cuts off its power."[19] The synergy that takes place when both men and women fulfill their callings and assignments according to the Lord's will is palpable. Sister Jean B. Bingham taught that combining the efforts of the Relief Society with the elders quorum "will bring unity that can yield astonishing results." Under the direction of the bishop, who holds presiding keys over the ward, "elders quorum and Relief Society presidencies can be inspired as they seek the best ways to watch over and care for each individual and family."[20]

One of the best ways for men and women to work together effectively is through councils. President M. Russell Ballard instructed: "Any priesthood leader who does not involve his sister leaders with full respect and inclusion is not honoring and magnifying the keys he has been given. His power and influence will be diminished until he learns the ways of the Lord."[21] Years ago, President Ballard related a conversation he had with the General President of the Relief Society. There was a question raised about strengthening the worthiness of youth preparing to serve missions. "President Elaine Jack said, 'You know, Elder Ballard, the [women] of the Church may have some good suggestions . . . if they [are] just asked. After all, . . . we *are* their mothers!'"[22]

For years the Brethren have encouraged priesthood leaders to involve women in councils. In 2015, the First Presidency and Quorum of the Twelve Apostles appointed the Relief Society General President to serve on the Priesthood and Family Executive Council (changing the council's name to make it more appropriate), the Young Women General President to serve on the Missionary Executive Council, and the Primary General President to serve on the Temple and Family History Executive Council. The First Presidency letter regarding the policy change stated, "We are confident that the wisdom and judgment of these general auxiliary presidents will provide a valuable dimension to the important work accomplished by these councils." [23]

Joan Chittister, a Catholic reporter on the topic of women's involvement in councils and meetings, stated, "Without the input of women, humanity sees with only one eye, hears with one ear and thinks with only one half of the human mind."[24] It is often easier and faster to counsel with only those with whom we agree, but coming to a consensus is not the reason for counseling—rather, it's to receive inspiration.

There is no question in my mind that the Lord would have us work together to establish Zion, strengthen families, and gather Israel. At the close of the historic general conference in which President Nelson repeated his plea to the sisters of the Church, declaring, "My dear sisters, we need *you*! We 'need *your* strength, *your* conversion, *your* conviction, *your* ability to lead, *your* wisdom, and *your* voices,'" he then added this important reason for why we are needed, "We simply cannot gather Israel without you."[25] We clearly need each other to accomplish the work of the Lord as men and women in this great work.

## SUSTAINING THOSE WITH PRIESTHOOD KEYS

As part of our Relief Society Declaration, we commit to "Sustain the priesthood of God on earth."[26] Sustaining the priesthood includes sustaining the men and women who hold and/or are authorized to use the priesthood, and perhaps especially those who hold priesthood keys. Although I feel that I have been immensely blessed by those who hold priesthood keys of presidency, I know that there are some women who have felt a little disheartened at times. When talking about sustaining key holders, one of the main questions I hear from women is, "How do I respond to a bishop or stake president when I put forth names for callings and they reject them, especially when I have fasted and prayed over them and have felt a confirmation regarding the individual?" I was asked that exact question the day before I gave a presentation on the topic of women and men and unity at church during Education Week. The morning I spoke, I went on a walk to get my final thoughts together and seek inspiration. While on the walk, I believe the Lord gave me a visual and real-life object lesson.

As I approached an elementary school, I watched three children approach the crosswalk. As they got closer, a car drew near, and the driver, noticing the children, stopped and let them cross. The two boys ran quickly across the street, but the younger girl, likely in kindergarten or first grade, was much slower. As she tried to speed up, she went off balance and fell off her scooter. During this time, a driver pulled up behind the car in front, and, seeing the boys run off, started honking the horn obnoxiously at the driver in front of him. With no motion from the first driver, the driver behind rolled down his window and began yelling for the front car to go. (I'm guessing he thought the driver ahead was on a cell phone and not paying attention.) The driver in front gave the driver behind no heed, but instead waited for the young girl to get back on her scooter and scoot across the street. By this time, I had walked close enough to both drivers to clearly see their expressions. The expression on the second driver's face as he realized his mistake was unforgettable. At that moment, I thought I heard a simple phrase come to my mind: "Your perspective changes depending on where you are sitting."

Those who hold keys are not perfect, but I have learned through experience that I need to give them the benefit of the doubt. They are the key holders. As president of an auxiliary, I may receive inspiration from the Lord, but my inspiration does not necessarily mean the person will be called. I do not know why decisions are made the way they are, but if I have a testimony of the calling of the key holder, I'm willing and happy to follow his leadership.

With regard to callings, *Handbook 2* states: "In some cases, priesthood and auxiliary leaders are asked to make recommendations to their stake presidency or bishopric. They should approach this responsibility prayerfully, knowing that they can receive guidance from the Lord about whom to recommend." Then this important instruction: "They should remember that final responsibility to receive inspiration on whom to call rests with the stake presidency or the bishopric." After the recommendations have been received, stake presidents and bishops are instructed to "carefully evaluate each recommendation, recognizing that it has been prayerfully considered."[27]

Reflecting on the early days of Nauvoo, historian Jill Derr explained, "The inclusion of women within the structure of the church organization reflected the divine pattern of the perfect union of man and woman, a pattern emphasized in the highest priesthood ordinances administered in the temple and essential to the restoration of the fullness of the priesthood."[28] In our day, President Nelson, speaking of the need for Relief Society sisters and priesthood holders to work together, declared, "We are complementary, not competitive partners in this work."[29]

## UNITY WITHIN THE FAMILY

It seems that there is something about having someone pass through the veil that reminds us of the importance of our covenants that allow us to be with our family members forever. On the headstone of my husband's parents are inscribed the words "No empty chairs," followed by the names of all of their children. On the back of my parents' headstone are the names of all their children as well. On the front of both of our parents' headstones is inscribed a picture of the Salt Lake Temple. As President Nelson taught:

> Brethren and sisters, material possessions and honors of the world do not endure. But your union as wife, husband, and family can. The only duration of family life that satisfies the loftiest longings of the human soul is forever. No sacrifice is too great to have the blessings of an eternal marriage. To qualify, one needs only to deny oneself of ungodliness and honor the ordinances of the temple. By making and keeping sacred temple covenants, we evidence our love for God, for our companion, and our real regard for our posterity—even those yet unborn. Our family is the focus of our greatest work and joy in this life; so will it be throughout all eternity, when we can "inherit thrones, kingdoms, principalities, . . . powers, dominions, . . . exaltation and glory" (D&C 132:19).[30]

## UNITY WITH CHRIST

Every baptized member of the Church is a covenant-making member. It is with Christ we covenant at baptism to mourn with those who mourn and comfort those who stand in need of comfort, and it is He whose commandments we promise to obey. Our covenants continue in the endowment as we covenant with Christ to strive more fully to become like Him. As we enter into the patriarchal order of the priesthood, we not only bind ourselves to our spouses, but we also covenant to do all we can to become like our Heavenly Parents as well as like Jesus Christ. The more we become like our Savior, the more we recognize how dependent we are on Him. This humility allows Him to help us become what we need to be, unified in Him, as He is with the Father.

My husband and I recently had our carpets cleaned by a gentleman from Peru who moved to the United States when he was eighteen. After he finished cleaning the carpets, we engaged in what I thought was simple small talk. I asked him about his family, his background, and his transition to the United States. He told me that when he first moved to Utah, he really struggled. There were so many temptations in the United States that did not exist in Peru, he related. "If it were not for the teachings of my mom, I would never would have made it, physically or spiritually." I asked what his mother did that made such an impact on his life. He responded with a story.

> The more we become like our Savior, the more we recognize how dependent we are on Him. This humility allows Him to help us become what we need to be, unified in Him, as He is with the Father.

When he was thirteen, living in Peru, his single mother began feeling that the animals in their neighborhood, especially the dogs, were being treated poorly, like garbage. In fact, she knew that people were literally throwing their dogs away in the garbage cans right before the garbage was being picked up. To resolve this concern, his mother took him and his younger brother to look through garbage cans around the city on the days the garbage was picked up. He called it the "dog rescuing mission." Over a six-month period, they rescued more than thirty dogs.

"What did you do with the dogs?" I asked.

"My mother loved animals," was his candid reply. "We kept every one of them."

One day, his mother decided that rather than going through garbage cans, it would be more effective if she and her two young sons went to the landfill where the garbage was dumped to rescue these dogs. He explained that the landfill in their city was massive and disgusting beyond imagination. The stench was almost unbearable, and there was absolutely nothing of value there. He remembered it being so dark in the landfill that at night he couldn't even see the stars in the sky. He knew his mother cared for dogs, but this seemed a bit drastic, in his young mind. Because of his great love and respect for his mother, however, and knowing of her pure motivation, he agreed to search for these unwanted dogs.

While he was walking through the landfill with his mom and brother, one particular sound caught their attention. They split up, trying to locate the place from where the sound originated. "The landfill was so large and it was so dark, the task was almost impossible," he explained. After searching for a long time, they realized the sound was near them, but muffled. They began digging through the trash and found, rather than another dog, tiny twin baby girls, only days old, buried in the landfill. "They were near dead," he explained, "starving and filthy. My mom immediately picked up the girls, cradled them in her arms, and wrapped them in her own clothes."

Engrossed in this incredible story, I inquired, "What happened to them? What did you do with them?"

"We brought them home, of course! You think my mom would bring home thirty dogs and give up these girls? They are my sisters!" He then explained, "For months, my mom thought she was being inspired to rescue dogs, but really, the Lord used her love for animals to put her in a position to find the rest of our family." Although they had little money, "my mother and the Lord somehow made it work." He then explained, "My mom and sisters are an inspiration to me. My mom lived every day to learn and act upon God's will, and my twin sisters live every day to the fullest knowing that their lives are a gift from God. My mom stayed true to the Lord and His Church throughout her life. All of my siblings are active in the Church. My mom taught us to listen to the Spirit and act. Her love, example, and teachings saved my life."

## CONCLUSION

The Prophet Joseph Smith taught that the purpose of the Relief Society was not just to relieve the poor but "to save souls." "Such is the end point of charity," he declared, "the pure love of Christ."[31] As we are unified with each other and especially with Christ, we will better fulfill God's work and glory, "to bring to pass the immortality and eternal life" (Moses 1:39) of His children. There is no competition but rather synergy as we bring our best gifts, strengths, and talents to the table and create harmony as one with the Lord. It is the Lord's power and authority we are privileged to use in behalf of others. Our job is to determine, with His help, how we can best use that power and authority to bless His children. As with the story of President Kimball and my parents, when we are unified with each other and the Lord, motivated with an eye single to His glory, empowered by the covenants we make with Him, and on His errand, we will be blessed to be a part of His work.

Chapter 7

# FILLING THE MEASURE OF OUR CREATION

From as early as I can remember, my siblings always had a paper route. By the time I was five, I started getting up early to help fold the papers, and by the age of six, I was helping deliver. As crazy as it sounds, I loved it! I loved walking around the neighborhood in the dark with my siblings and eventually doing so with just my dad. When I became a teenager, however, one day my dad slipped and fell on the early-morning ice, broke his leg, and was thus unable to help. I started doing the route alone. One dark morning, as I was turning the corner at the end of one of the streets in my neighborhood, a white van pulled up to me and a man opened up the side door and yelled at me to get in. Within seconds, our blue minivan screeched up right behind the white van, and my mother yelled for me to get in. I ran immediately for her van, jumped in, and slammed the door, and both my mother and the white van took off—in opposite directions. I sat in silence, filled with panic and awe, as we drove home. Once we pulled into our driveway, we looked at each other, and without my saying a word to her, my mom said, "I just knew..."

Although she was usually awake in the early hours, my mom was typically busy making breakfast, helping the older kids get out the door in time for early-morning seminary, doing dishes, and so on. Not once, prior to that occasion, do I remember her ever just meeting me on the route unexpectedly. "It would be impossible to measure the influence that such women have, not only on families but also on the Lord's Church, as wives, mothers, and grandmothers; as sisters and aunts; as teachers and leaders; and especially as exemplars and devout defenders of the faith," President Russell M. Nelson declared. "This has been true in every gospel dispensation since the days of Adam and Eve. Yet the women of this dispensation are distinct from the women of any other because this dispensation is distinct from any other. This distinction brings both privileges and responsibilities." Adding then to the prophetic pleadings of previous Church leaders, President Nelson said: "We need women who know how to make important things happen by their faith and who are courageous defenders of morality and families in a sin-sick world. We need women who are devoted to shepherding God's children along the covenant path toward exaltation; women who know how to receive personal revelation, who understand the power and peace of the temple endowment; women who know how to call upon the powers of heaven to protect and strengthen children and families."[1]

> "The women of this dispensation are distinct from the women of any other because this dispensation is distinct from any other. This distinction brings both privileges and responsibilities."
> —RUSSELL M. NELSON

My mom did this in her way, but, as covenant-keeping women, we all have our own missions, our own responsibilities, and our own gifts and talents. No two of us are alike. President Nelson explained that each woman has "special spiritual gifts and propensities." He urged us, "with all the hope of [his] heart, to pray to understand *your spiritual gifts*—to cultivate, use, and expand them, even more than you ever have. You will change the world as you do so."[2]

Elder Dieter F. Uchtdorf used the following parable to help men better lay hold on their priesthood privileges. As the principles apply to women as well, I have taken the liberty to change the gender in the quotation and add a little feminine touch.

There once was a woman whose lifelong dream was to board a cruise ship and sail the Mediterranean Sea. She dreamed of walking the streets of Rome, Athens, and Istanbul. She saved every penny until she had enough for her passage. Since money was tight, she brought an extra suitcase filled with cans of beans, boxes of crackers, and bags of powdered lemonade, and that is what she lived on every day.

She would have loved to take part in the many activities offered on the ship—working out in the gym, [relaxing in the spa], and swimming in the pool. She envied those who went to movies, shows, and cultural presentations. And, oh, how she yearned for only a taste of the amazing food she saw on the ship—every meal appeared to be a feast! But the woman wanted to spend so very little money that she didn't participate in any of these. She was able to see the cities she had longed to visit, but for the most part of the journey, she stayed in her cabin and ate only her humble food.

On the last day of the cruise, a crew member asked her which of the farewell parties she would be attending. It was then that the woman learned that not only the farewell party but almost everything on board the cruise ship—the food, the entertainment, all the activities—had been included in the price of her ticket. Too late the woman realized that she had been living far beneath her privileges.[3]

Many Church members, not knowing what blessings they have access to and what privileges are theirs, go through mortality not taking full advantage of the spiritual feast and powers available to them. They are thus minimizing the influence they could have on others. This is especially true when it comes to women and the priesthood. We are living in a day and age when equality, power, fairness, and tolerance are touted above other virtues. Identity, authority, spirituality, and even God are topics of great confusion for many; others are not troubled over these issues at all, and they often find themselves perplexed or frustrated by those who do. Regardless of where we stand, the more we understand and take advantage of our priesthood privileges, the more influence for good we will have.

Every woman and man born on this earth has been blessed with the light of Christ and has the ability to be influenced by the Holy Ghost. Every baptized member has been exhorted to receive the Holy Ghost, and every covenant-keeping member possesses that gift. Through the power of the Holy Ghost, we can know the will of God for us. "You do not have to wonder if you are where the Lord needs you to be or if you are doing what He needs you to do," President Nelson instructed. "You can know! The Holy Ghost will tell you 'all things what ye should do.'"[4] As we make and keep sacred covenants and are obedient to the will of the Lord, reaching out for more guidance and power and strength, He will give it to us. As we enter the temple, we participate in ordinances and make covenants with the Lord that, if we keep them, increase our spiritual capacity and the power of God in our lives. We are literally endowed with power to know and do God's will and thwart the adversary. As we go about God's work, we will have not only angels beside us but God as well.

President M. Russell Ballard explained:

> Women of the Church [need] to know the doctrine of Christ and to bear testimony of the Restoration in every way that you can. Never has there been a more complex time in the history of the earth. . . . We need more of the distinctive, influential voices and faith of women. We need you to learn the doctrine and to understand what we believe so that you can bear your testimonies about the truth of all things—whether those testimonies be given around a campfire at girls' camp, in a testimony meeting, in a blog, or on Facebook. Only you can show the world what women of God who have made covenants look like and believe.[5]

I often long for more covenant-keeping women to understand and act upon this truth. Our youth and young adults, especially our females, desperately need covenant-keeping women to talk to, teach them, and guide them in the right direction. They need covenant-keeping women whom they can trust not only to have strong opinions but to be basing their opinions on gospel truth. They need covenant-keeping women who understand the temptations and difficulties of our times and know how to make critical decisions based on gospel principles and doctrines. I am concerned at times with the "spiritual Twinkies" being offered to our young women. Our young women do not need more quotes from Facebook or insights coming from popular social media sites or Google—they need truth from scriptures testified of through experience. Our young women do not need to be entertained; they need to be built up in their faith. They need mentors grounded in the teachings and experiences provided by God, teachers who understand their priesthood privileges and use them.

In our day, women are given a variety of choices and options that have not been available in times past. This is an incredible time for women, and the Lord needs us. He needs us to be the best we can be, in our own spheres, capitalizing on our own gifts and talents, and becoming even stronger influences for good in the Lord's kingdom. "One sister," explained President Ballard, "may be inspired to continue her education and attend medical school, allowing her to have significant impact on her patients and to advance medical research. For another sister, inspiration may lead her to forgo a scholarship to a prestigious institution and instead begin a family much earlier than has become common in this generation, allowing her to make a significant and eternal impact on her children now. Is it possible for two similarly faithful women to receive such different responses to the same basic questions? Absolutely!" He concluded, "What's right for one woman may not be right for another."[6]

I love studying the lives of the prophets. I admit that I love studying the wives of the prophets as well. I love that President Nelson and President Oaks are currently married to women, Wendy Watson Nelson and Kristen McMain Oaks, who both have PhDs and were both university professors. I also love that their deceased wives, Dantzel White Nelson and June Dixon Oaks, were not. I love that Sister Dantzel Nelson gave up a scholarship to Juilliard but still sang in the Tabernacle Choir while raising ten children. I love that Sister Ruth L. Renlund worked full time as a successful attorney while her husband was a heart surgeon. They both fulfilled significant callings, raised a daughter, supported each other, and kept their covenants. I love that our women's general auxiliary leaders are diverse in their cultures, marital status, views, and employment experiences. What a blessing to have women leaders and mentors from all walks of life! Too often, gender can be used as an excuse, whether intentional or not, for limiting our ability to fill the measure of our creation. Rather than putting limits on ourselves and others, we need to expand our possibilities.

As a young seminary student, I asked a leader what I needed to do to become a full-time seminary teacher. "I'm so sorry, but you can't," came the reply. "They don't hire women to teach full time." Imagine my excitement when I was later hired as a full-time seminary teacher. I remember as a full-time seminary teacher asking if it was possible to coordinate on the East Coast. "No," came the uninformed response. "You need the priesthood to be a coordinator, especially in the East." Again, imagine my surprise when I was asked to serve as the institute director and seminary coordinator in the Boston, Massachusetts, area. Imagine my surprise when I also learned that I would be the Latter-day Saint chaplain at Harvard and MIT. I had wrongly assumed that being ordained to the priesthood was necessary for that assignment. I was not shocked that both Church members and those not of our faith tradition were surprised to have a woman serving as a chaplain. Frankly, I was too! There was no change in policy; it just simply hadn't ever happened before.

When we limit a woman's ability to serve based on misunderstanding priesthood roles and offices, we not only add to the confusion, but we also hinder progress for individuals, families, and the Church. The Brethren are pleading with the sisters to do more, to teach more, and to lead more. Just because women haven't done certain things before, that doesn't mean it can never happen in the future. Women now pray at general conference, sit in prominent positions on the stand at general conference, run the humanitarian program of the Church, serve in full-time missionary leadership positions, sit in the general councils of the Church, and much more.

## WOMEN OF THE CHURCH ARE TO LEAD WOMEN OF THE WORLD

President Joseph F. Smith instructed the sisters: "It is not for you to be led by the women of the world; it is for you to lead . . . the women of the world, in everything that is praise-worthy, everything that is God-like, everything that is uplifting and that is purifying to the children of men."[7] Sister Belle S. Spafford, Relief Society General President from 1945 to 1974, spoke on the enhancement of opportunities for women in the world. After going through a brief history of the opportunities women have received since the organization of the Relief Society, she declared: "Today a woman's world is as broad as the universe. There's scarcely an area of human endeavor that a woman cannot enter if she has the will and preparation to do so."[8]

In 2001, President Gordon B. Hinckley told the young women of the Church: "The whole gamut of human endeavor is now open to women. There is not anything that you cannot do if you will set your mind to it. You can include in the dream of the woman you would like to be a picture of one qualified to serve society and make a significant contribution to the world of which she will be a part."[9] While speaking at a National Press Club event in Washington, DC, President Hinckley acknowledged that "people wonder what we do for our women." He then declared, "I will tell you what we do: we get out of their way and look with wonder at what they are accomplishing."[10]

I have been amazed at our sisters who follow the Spirit as they raise families; serve in callings; provide service in politics and other government positions; and work in journalism, medicine, humanities, education, law, and so much more. They are leading the women of the world. Eliza R. Snow said that Latter-day Saint women "have greater and higher privileges than any other females upon the face of the earth."[11] Sheri Dew explained, "This is because the temple gives [Latter-day Saint] women spiritual privileges no other women on earth may claim."[12]

President Spencer W. Kimball reminded us: "In the world before we came here, faithful women were given certain assignments while faithful men were foreordained to certain priesthood tasks. While we do not now remember the particulars, this does not alter the glorious reality of what we once agreed to. You are accountable for those things which long ago were expected of you just as are those we sustain as prophets and apostles!"[13] I've often wondered what I agreed to in the premortal realm. Like many women, I'm concerned I may have agreed to much more than was humanly possible. Although I'm likely falling short in many areas, I constantly pray that I will remember and do those things that are of greatest value and import to the Lord.

Sister Linda S. Reeves, former counselor in the Relief Society General Presidency and mother of thirteen, related that a friend once cautioned her: "When you ask the sisters to read the scriptures and pray more, it stresses them out. They already feel like they have too much to do." Sister Reeves responded: "Brothers and sisters, because I know from my own experiences, and those of my husband, I must testify of the blessings of daily scripture study and prayer and weekly family home evening. These are the very practices that help take away stress, give direction to our lives, and add protection to our homes."[14] In our day, not only is the Lord, through His prophets, teaching empowering truths to and regarding women, it seems that He is enhancing our ability as well. While the world perhaps seems to be expecting less and less, the Lord seems to be expecting more and more. The "more" that the Lord requires, however, is that which is most important—in fact, it's the very purpose for which we are here.

## CONCLUSION

President Russell M. Nelson taught: "To help another human being reach one's celestial potential is part of the divine mission of woman. As mother, teacher, or nurturing saint, she molds living clay to the shape of her hopes. In partnership with God, her divine mission is to help spirits live and souls be lifted. This is the measure of her creation. It is ennobling, edifying, and exalting."[15] This is precisely what Joseph Smith taught the early Relief Society sisters as he prepared them to enter the holy temple. This is what our prophet is pleading for us to do today: "Take your rightful and needful place in your home, in your community, and in the kingdom of God—more than you ever have before."[16]

Whoever we are, whatever our current situation, no matter how much or little we've done in the past, the Lord is asking for more. Our prophet has blessed us, using the keys of the holy priesthood and apostleship, "to rise to [our] full stature, to fulfill the measure of [our] creation, as we walk arm in arm in this sacred work. Together we will help prepare the world for the Second Coming of the Lord."[17] I have no question that women, armed with the priesthood power and authority with which they have been set apart and endowed, can fulfill this prophetic vision. May each of us live up to our God-given privileges under both the hierarchical and patriarchal orders of the priesthood.

# ACKNOWLEDGMENTS

I will forever thank my mother for her drilling into her children the importance of inclusiveness. That being said, the hardest part of being inclusive is recognizing that some people, for a variety of reasons, get left out at times. Knowing that, I acknowledge up front my gratitude for so many, named and unnamed, for your help, example, questions, answers, and inspiration that helped in creating this book. I recognize that most of the important work we do in this world comes as a result of being able to stand on another's shoulders.

That being said, there are a number of people I would like to acknowledge specifically in the creation of this book. My parents, siblings, in-laws, aunts, ward members, presidencies, teachers, close friends, students, colleagues, and assistants have been most influential in allowing me to pester them over the years with questions, ideas, and experiences. They have responded with stories, more questions, and thoughtful insights. I truly believe we are each other's "clinical material," and I'm grateful for all those who have been placed in my path.

Special thanks to Jennifer Morgan, my sister-in-law, who with enthusiasm, intrigue, and confidence not only encouraged me in the writing of the book but read draft after draft, providing me with pragmatic insights, questions, and support. Rick Gardner, my brother-in-law, also enthusiastically helped with graphics, as did the computer support team in the BYU Religion Department.

Throughout this effort, I was blessed with many colleagues who gave

## ACKNOWLEDGMENTS

continued support. Frank Judd, from his office across the hall from mine, reminded me constantly and enthusiastically about the importance of the message and provided, through his optimism and continued follow-up, the confidence and drive I needed to continue the project. Brent Top, Max Molgard, Dan Judd, Richard Cowan, and Bob Millet allowed and even encouraged me to bombard their lives with questions, and they eagerly responded with more references, thoughtful responses, and careful and mature guidance.

The wise and thoughtful conversations I was blessed to be a part of with Camille Fronk Olson, Jill Derr, Sharon Eubank, Sheri Dew, Sydney Reynolds, and Virginia Pearce Cowley were critical and foundational to this book. Their experiences, insights, wisdom, questions, and knowledge, motivated by their intense and pure desire to understand and serve effectively, will always be an inspiration to me.

The feedback, confidence, editing, and constant encouragement of my Deseret Book team cannot go unnoticed. This book simply would not exist without the encouragement, hard work, brilliance, and determination of Lisa Roper. She is a rock star! Laurel Christensen Day, Reid Neilson, Kathy Hughes, and others provided critical feedback. Emily Watts has taken the book from where it was and made it better.

My sincerest gratitude goes to my husband, Dustin Gardner. His character, commitment, support, and love are more than anything I could have imagined. I'm beyond grateful to have a husband who walks hand in hand with me, side by side on this covenant path.

# NOTES

INTRODUCTION: "FOR SUCH A TIME AS THIS"

1. Thomas S. Monson, "Welcome to Conference," *Ensign,* November 2012.
2. Russell M. Nelson and Wendy W. Nelson, "Hope of Israel," Worldwide Youth Devotional, June 3, 2018; broadcasts.churchofjesuschrist.org.
3. M. Russell Ballard, "Let Us Think Straight," Brigham Young University Devotional, August 20, 2013; speeches.byu.edu.
4. Lynn A. McKinlay, "Patriarchal Order of the Priesthood," in *Encyclopedia of Mormonism,* 4 vols., ed. Daniel H. Ludlow (New York: Macmillan, 1992), 1:1067.
5. Dallin H. Oaks, "The Keys and Authority of the Priesthood," *Ensign,* May 2014.
6. During his opening remarks in the October 2018 general conference, President Nelson said, "As Latter-day Saints, we have become accustomed to thinking of 'church' as something that happens in our meetinghouses, supported by what happens at home. *We need an adjustment to this pattern.*" Russell M. Nelson, "Opening Remarks," *Ensign,* November 2018; emphasis added.
7. Sheri Dew, *Women and the Priesthood: What One Mormon Woman Believes* (Salt Lake City: Deseret Book, 2013), 7–10.
8. Jeffrey R. Holland, "Be Not Afraid, Only Believe," Evening with a General Authority, February 6, 2015; broadcasts.churchofjesuschrist.org.
9. Dew, *Women and the Priesthood,* 7, 9–10.
10. Russell M. Nelson, "Revelation for the Church, Revelation for Our Lives," *Ensign,* May 2018; Neal A. Maxwell, "Meek and Lowly," Brigham Young University Devotional, October 21, 1986; speeches.byu.edu.
11. Nelson, "Revelation."
12. Bruce R. McConkie, "The Doctrine of the Priesthood," *Ensign,* May 1982.
13. Boyd K. Packer, "Little Children," *Ensign,* November 1986.
14. Russell M. Nelson, "A Plea to My Sisters," *Ensign,* November 2015.

# NOTES

15. Heber C. Kimball, in *Journal of Discourses* (London: Latter-day Saints' Book Depot, 1865), 10:167; emphasis added.
16. Nelson, "Revelation."

## CHAPTER 1: DOCTRINE, HISTORY, AND STRUCTURE OF THE PRIESTHOOD

1. Edward L. Kimball and Andrew E. Kimball Jr., *Spencer W. Kimball* (Salt Lake City: Bookcraft, 1977), 334.
2. M. Russell Ballard, "This Is My Work and Glory," *Ensign*, May 2013.
3. Ezra Taft Benson, "What I Hope You Will Teach Your Children about the Temple," *Ensign*, August 1985.
4. Russell M. Nelson, "Ministering with the Power and Authority of God," *Ensign*, May 2018.
5. Dale G. Renlund and Ruth Lybbert Renlund, *The Melchizedek Priesthood: Understanding the Doctrine, Living the Principles* (Salt Lake City: Deseret Book, 2018), 11–12.
6. Renlund and Renlund, *Melchizedek Priesthood*, 12.
7. Dallin H. Oaks, "Priesthood Authority in the Family and the Church," *Ensign*, November 2005.
8. John Godfrey Saxe, *The Poems of John Godfrey Saxe* (Boston: James R. Osgood, 1873), 135–36, books.google.com.
9. Julie B. Beck, Brigham Young University Women's Conference address, April 29, 2011.
10. Erastus Snow, in *Journal of Discourses*, 26 vols. (London: Latter-day Saints' Book Depot, 1878), 19:269–70.
11. Dallin H. Oaks, "Apostasy and Restoration," *Ensign*, May 1995.
12. Harold B. Lee, *The Teachings of Harold B. Lee* (Salt Lake City: Bookcraft, 1996), 22.
13. M. Russell Ballard, "The Opportunities and Responsibilities of CES Teachers in the 21st Century," Evening with a General Authority, February 26, 2016, broadcasts.churchofjesuschrist.org.
14. John A. Widtsoe, "Everlasting Motherhood," *Millennial Star* 90, no. 19 (May 10, 1928), 298.
15. Glenn L. Pace, "The Divine Nature and Destiny of Women," Brigham Young University Devotional, March 6, 2010; speeches.byu.edu.
16. Russell M. Nelson, "Nurturing Marriage," *Ensign*, May 2006.
17. Oaks, "Priesthood Authority."
18. Robert L. Millet, "Restoring the Patriarchal Order," Brigham Young University Family Expo address, April 1998.
19. "The Family: A Proclamation to the World," *Ensign*, November 2010.
20. *Teachings of Presidents of the Church: Joseph Smith* (Salt Lake City: The Church of Jesus Christ of Latter-day Saints, 2007), 40.
21. Wilford Woodruff, in *Journal of Discourses*, 4:192.
22. Woodruff, in *Journal of Discourses*, 4:192.
23. Brigham Young, in *Journal of Discourses*, 6:275.

NOTES

24. James E. Talmage, "The Eternity of Sex," *Young Woman's Journal* 25, no. 10 (October 1914): 602–3.
25. *Teachings: Joseph Smith*, 482. See also Moses 3:18–25; Abraham 5:14–21.
26. Henry B. Eyring, "Women and Gospel Learning in the Home," *Ensign*, November 2018.
27. *Teachings: Joseph Smith*, 105.
28. Ezra Taft Benson, "What I Hope You Will Teach Your Children about the Temple," *Ensign*, August 1985.
29. Benson, "What I Hope."
30. Russell M. Nelson, *The Power within Us* (Salt Lake City: Deseret Book, 1988), 109.
31. Ezra Taft Benson, "What I Hope."
32. Bruce R. McConkie, "Our Sisters from the Beginning," *Ensign*, January 1979.
33. Millet, "Restoring the Patriarchal Order."
34. Bruce R. McConkie, *A New Witness for the Articles of Faith* (Salt Lake City: Deseret Book, 1985), 35.
35. Ezra Taft Benson, "What I Hope," 9.
36. Bruce R. McConkie, "Patriarchal Order—Eternal Family Concept," 1967 BYU Religion lecture. Transcription in possession of the author.
37. Joseph Fielding Smith, *Doctrines of Salvation*, 3 vols. (Salt Lake City: Bookcraft, 1954–56), 2:165; Bruce R. McConkie, *Doctrinal New Testament Commentary*, 3 vols. (Salt Lake City: Bookcraft, 1965), 1:400.
38. Russell M. Nelson, "Keys of the Priesthood," *Ensign*, October 2005.
39. With the possible exception of John the Baptist and the Three Nephites.
40. Renlund and Renlund, *Melchizedek Priesthood*, 14.
41. Renlund and Renlund, *Melchizedek Priesthood*, 14–15.
42. *Teachings: Joseph Smith*, 104.
43. Joseph Fielding Smith, *Doctrines of Salvation*, 3:126–27.
44. *Teachings: Joseph Smith*, 310.
45. *Teachings: Joseph Smith*, 311.
46. Ezra Taft Benson, "What I Hope"; emphasis added.
47. *Teachings: Joseph Smith*, 419.
48. M. Russell Ballard, "Women of Dedication, Faith, Determination, and Action," Brigham Young University Women's Conference address, May 1, 2015.
49. Boyd K. Packer, "The Power of the Priesthood," *Ensign*, May 2010.
50. Russell M. Nelson, "Lessons from Eve," *Ensign*, November 1987.

CHAPTER 2: PRIESTHOOD KEYS, AUTHORITY, AND POWER IN THE CHURCH

1. Dallin H. Oaks, "Priesthood Authority in the Family and the Church," *Ensign*, November 2005.
2. *Gospel Principles* (Salt Lake City: The Church of Jesus Christ of Latter-day Saints, 2009), 75–77.

# NOTES

3. M. Russell Ballard, "Men and Women in the Work of the Lord," *New Era*, April 2014. See also *Daughters in My Kingdom: The History and Work of Relief Society* (Salt Lake City: The Church of Jesus Christ of Latter-day Saints, 2011), 138.
4. Dallin H. Oaks, "The Keys and Authority of the Priesthood," *Ensign*, May 2014.
5. Russell M. Nelson, "Keys of the Priesthood," *Ensign*, October 2005.
6. *Handbook 2: Administering the Church* (Salt Lake City: The Church of Jesus Christ of Latter-day Saints, 2010), 2.1.1; emphasis added.
7. *Handbook 2*, 2.1.1.
8. *Handbook 2*, 2.1.1.
9. *Handbook 2*, 2.1.1.
10. *Doctrine and Covenants and Church History Study Guide for Home-Study Seminary Students* (Salt Lake City: The Church of Jesus Christ of Latter-day Saints, 2017), 410.
11. *Handbook 2*, 2.1.1.
12. *Doctrine and Covenants Home-Study*, 410.
13. *Handbook 2*, 2.1.1.
14. *Handbook 2*, 2.1.1.
15. *Doctrine and Covenants Home-Study*, 410.
16. Dallin H. Oaks, "The Aaronic Priesthood and the Sacrament," *Ensign*, November 1998.
17. M. Russell Ballard, "Let Us Think Straight," Brigham Young University Devotional, August 20, 2013; speeches.byu.edu.
18. *Doctrine and Covenants Home-Study*, 410.
19. Donald L. Hallstrom, "Strengthening the Family and the Church through the Priesthood," Worldwide Leadership Training Meeting, 2013; broadcasts.churchofjesuschrist.org.
20. Dallin H. Oaks, *The Lord's Way* (Salt Lake City: Deseret Book, 1991), 68–69.
21. Ezra Booth, *Painesville Telegraph*, December 20, 1831, cited in Lyndon W. Cook, *The Revelations of the Prophet Joseph Smith* (Salt Lake City: Deseret Book, 1985), 61–62.
22. Marion G. Romney, in Conference Report, October 1960, 76–77.
23. Dale G. Renlund, "That I Might Draw All Men unto Me," *Ensign*, May 2016.
24. Russell M. Nelson, "Drawing the Power of Jesus Christ into Our Lives," *Ensign*, April 2017.
25. Neal A. Maxwell, *Things as They Really Are* (Salt Lake City: Deseret Book) 1980, xii.
26. Nelson, "Drawing the Power."
27. Julie B. Beck, Brigham Young University Women's Conference address, May 2011.
28. Russell M. Nelson, "The Price of Priesthood Power," *Ensign*, May 2016.
29. The Joseph Smith Papers, "Nauvoo Relief Society Minute Book," p. [61];

# NOTES

https://www.josephsmithpapers.org/paper-summary/nauvoo-relief-society-minute-book/58.

CHAPTER 3: "WHAT OTHER AUTHORITY CAN IT BE?"
CONNECTING WOMEN WITH PRIESTHOOD AT CHURCH

1. Neil L. Andersen, "Power in the Priesthood," *Ensign,* November 2013.
2. Dallin H. Oaks, "Strengthening the Family," broadcasts.churchofjesuschrist.org.
3. M. Russell Ballard, "Let Us Think Straight," Brigham Young University Devotional, August 20, 2013; speeches.byu.edu; Joseph Fielding Smith, "Magnifying Our Callings in the Priesthood," *Improvement Era,* June 1970, 66; emphasis added. For a more in-depth discussion on the blessings of the priesthood, see Bruce R. McConkie, "The Ten Blessings of the Priesthood," *Ensign,* November 1977.
4. Dallin H. Oaks, "Priesthood Authority in the Family and the Church," *Ensign,* November 2005.
5. Oaks, "Priesthood Authority."
6. Russell M. Nelson, "Let Us All Press On," *Ensign,* May 2018.
7. Oaks, "Priesthood Authority."
8. Oaks, "Priesthood Authority."
9. Oaks, "Priesthood Authority."
10. Russell M. Nelson, *Teachings of Russell M. Nelson* (Salt Lake City: Deseret Book, 2018), 199–200.
11. Dale G. Renlund and Ruth Lybbert Renlund, *The Melchizedek Priesthood: Understanding the Doctrine, Living the Principles* (Salt Lake City: Deseret Book, 2018), 18–20.
12. Russell M. Nelson, "A Plea to My Sisters," *Ensign,* November 2015, note 7; Joseph Fielding Smith, "Relief Society—An Aid to the Priesthood," *Relief Society Magazine,* January 1959, 51.
13. Nelson, "A Plea to My Sisters."
14. Sara M. Kimball, "Auto-Biography," *Woman's Exponent,* vol. 12, no. 7 (September 1, 1883): 51.
15. The Joseph Smith Papers, "History, 1838–1856, volume C-1 [2 November 1838–31 July 1842]," 1326; https://josephsmithpapers.org/paper-summary/history-1838-1856-volume-c-1-2-november-1838-31-july-1842/500.
16. Dallin H. Oaks, "The Relief Society and the Church," *Ensign,* May 1992.
17. *Daughters in My Kingdom: The History and Work of Relief Society* (Salt Lake City: The Church of Jesus Christ of Latter-day Saints, 2011), 7; Eliza R. Snow, "Female Relief Society," *Deseret News,* April 22, 1868, 1.
18. Oaks, "Relief Society," 35; The Joseph Smith Papers, "Nauvoo Relief Society Minute Book," p. [40]; https://www.josephsmithpapers.org/paper-summary/nauvoo-relief-society-minute-book/37.
19. Bonnie L. Oscarson, "Rise Up in Strength, Sisters in Zion," *Ensign,* November 2016.

NOTES

20. *Handbook 2: Administering the Church* (Salt Lake City: The Church of Jesus Christ of Latter-day Saints, 2010), 5.1; see also 4.5, 6.1.
21. Boyd K. Packer, "The Relief Society," *Ensign,* May 1998.
22. Dallin H. Oaks, *Life's Lessons Learned: Personal Reflections* (Salt Lake City: Deseret Book, 2011), 69.
23. Ballard, "Let Us Think Straight," 5.

CHAPTER 4: THE TEMPLE AND THE PATRIARCHAL ORDER OF THE PRIESTHOOD

1. Boyd K. Packer, *The Holy Temple* (Salt Lake City: Bookcraft, 1980), 264–65.
2. Packer, *The Holy Temple,* 264–65.
3. Spencer W. Kimball, "Marriage Is Honorable," Brigham Young University Devotional, September 30, 1973; speeches.byu.edu.
4. Ezra Taft Benson, "What I Hope You Will Teach Your Children about the Temple," *Ensign,* August 1985.
5. The Joseph Smith Papers, "History, 1838–1856, volume E-1 [1 July 1843–30 April 1844]," 1708; https://www.josephsmithpapers.org/paper-summary/history-1838-1856-volume-e-1-1-july-1843-30-april-1844/80.
6. *Teachings of Presidents of the Church: Joseph Smith* (Salt Lake City: The Church of Jesus Christ of Latter-day Saints, 2007), 510.
7. George Q. Cannon, in *Journal of Discourses,* 26 vols. (London: Latter-day Saints' Book Depot, 1884), 25:289.
8. *Teachings: Joseph Smith,* 416.
9. *Teachings: Joseph Smith,* 414.
10. Jill Mulvay Derr, Janath Russell Cannon, and Maureen Ursenback Beecher, *Women of Covenant: The Story of Relief Society* (Salt Lake City: Deseret Book, 1992), 1.
11. Derr, Cannon, and Beecher, *Women of Covenant,* 1.
12. Derr, Cannon, and Beecher, *Women of Covenant,* 1.
13. Derr, Cannon, and Beecher, *Women of Covenant,* 45.
14. Lynn A. McKinlay, "Patriarchal Order of the Priesthood," in *Encyclopedia of Mormonism,* 4 vols., ed. Daniel H. Ludlow (New York: Macmillan, 1992), 1:1067.
15. Russell M. Nelson, "The Atonement," address given at the seminar for new mission presidents, June 25, 2002, Church History Library, Salt Lake City.
16. Bruce R. McConkie, *A New Witness for the Articles of Faith* (Salt Lake City: Deseret Book, 1985), 315.
17. M. Russell Ballard, "Let Us Think Straight," Brigham Young University Devotional, August 20, 2013; speeches.byu.edu.
18. Allen Claire Rozsa, "Temple Ordinances," in *Encyclopedia of Mormonism,* 1:1444.
19. https://www.churchofjesuschrist.org/topics/garments?lang=eng.
20. https://www.churchofjesuschrist.org/church/news/church-produces-video-on-sacred-nature-and-purpose-of-temple-garments?lang=eng&_r=1.

# NOTES

21. Robert D. Hales, *Return: Four Phases of Our Mortal Journey Home* (Salt Lake City: Deseret Book, 2010), 246.
22. Sheri Dew and Virginia H. Pearce, *The Beginning of Better Days* (Salt Lake: Deseret Book, 2012), 26–27.
23. Ballard, "Let Us Think Straight"; John A. Widtsoe, *Priesthood and Church Government* (Salt Lake City: Deseret Book, 1939), 83; *Joseph Smith* (Salt Lake City: Bookcraft, 1980), 140n.
24. Brigham Young, *Discourses of Brigham Young,* sel. John A. Widtsoe (Salt Lake City: Deseret Book, 1954), 416.
25. Alma P. Burton, "The Endowment," in *Encyclopedia of Mormonism,* 1:1067.
26. James E. Talmage, *The House of the Lord: A Study of Holy Sanctuaries Ancient and Modern* (Salt Lake City: The Church of Jesus Christ of Latter-day Saints, 1912), 84.
27. www.churchofjesuschrist.org/media-library/video/2014-01-1460-sacred-temple-clothing?lang=eng&_r=1.
28. Young, *Discourses of Brigham Young,* 161.
29. Sheri Dew, *Women and the Priesthood* (Salt Lake City: Deseret Book, 2013), 126; Doctrine and Covenants 76:8; 38:39; Alma 12:9.
30. Russell M. Nelson, "A Plea to My Sisters," *Ensign,* November 2015.
31. Talmage, *House of the Lord,* 153; 1 Corinthians 11:11.
32. Talmage, *House of the Lord,* 153; 1 Corinthians 11:11.
33. Joseph Fielding Smith, *Doctrines of Salvation,* 3 vols., comp. Bruce R. McConkie (Salt Lake City: Bookcraft, 1955), 2:44.
34. Cree-L Kofford, "Marriage in the Lord's Way," *Ensign,* June 1998.
35. Bruce R. McConkie, in Conference Report, September 1950, 15–16.
36. Dale G. Renlund and Ruth Lybbert Renlund, *The Melchizedek Priesthood: Understanding the Doctrine, Living the Principles* (Salt Lake City: Deseret Book, 2018), 20.
37. Bruce R. McConkie, "Patriarchal Order—Eternal Family Concept," 1967 BYU Religion lecture. Transcription in possession of the author.
38. Packer, *The Holy Temple,* 181–82; John A. Widtsoe, "The House of the Lord," *Improvement Era,* April 1936, 228.
39. Henry B. Eyring, "Hearts Bound Together," *Ensign,* May 2005.
40. Russell M. Nelson, "Sisters' Participation in the Gathering of Israel," *Ensign,* November 2018.
41. Dallin H. Oaks, "Taking upon Us the Name of Jesus Christ," *Ensign,* May 1985; emphasis added.
42. Bruce R. McConkie, "Our Sisters from the Beginning," *Ensign,* January 1979.
43. *Teachings of Presidents of the Church: Brigham Young* (Salt Lake City: The Church of Jesus Christ of Latter-day Saints, 1997), 138.
44. *Handbook 2: Administering the Church* (Salt Lake City: The Church of Jesus Christ of Latter-day Saints, 2010), 2.1.1.
45. Packer, *The Holy Temple,* 151.

46. Boyd K. Packer, "What Every Elder Should Know—And Every Sister as Well," *Ensign*, February 1993.
47. Russell M. Nelson, "Ministering with the Power and Authority of God," *Ensign*, May 2018.
48. Ballard, "Let Us Think Straight"; Widtsoe, *Priesthood and Church Government*, 83.
49. The Joseph Smith Papers, "Nauvoo Relief Society Minute Book," p. [40]; https://www.josephsmithpapers.org/paper-summary/nauvoo-relief-society-minute-book/37.
50. Ballard, "Let Us Think Straight."
51. D. Todd Christofferson, "The Power of Covenants," *Ensign*, May 2009.
52. Tad R. Callister, "Our Identity and Our Destiny," Brigham Young University Devotional, August 14, 2012; speeches.byu.edu.
53. Packer, *The Holy Temple*, 178–79; George Q. Cannon, "The Logan Temple," *Millennial Star*, vol. 39, no. 46 (November 12, 1877), 743.
54. Linda K. Burton, "Priesthood: 'A Sacred Trust to Be Used for the Benefit of Men, Women, and Children,'" Brigham Young University Women's Conference address, May 3, 2013.
55. Russell M. Nelson, "Symbols and the Temple," St. Louis Missouri Temple dedication, June 5, 1997.
56. Thomas S. Monson, "The Holy Temple—a Beacon to the World," *Ensign*, May 2011.
57. Gordon B. Hinckley, "Some Thoughts on Temples, Retention of Converts, and Missionary Service," *Ensign*, November 1997.
58. Ballard, "Let Us Think Straight."
59. Carol F. McConkie, "Receive Heavenly Power in the Temple," LDS Business College Devotional, May 1, 2012; https://www.ldsbc.edu/receive-heavenly-power-in-the-temple.
60. Russell M. Nelson, "Teachings, Covenants, Signs," Salt Lake Temple Devotional, October 11, 1998.
61. Dale G. Renlund, "Family History and Temple Work: Sealing and Healing," *Ensign*, May 2018.
62. Russell M. Nelson, "As We Go Forward Together," *Ensign*, April 2018.
63. Packer, *The Holy Temple*, 181–82; Widtsoe, "The House of the Lord," 228.
64. Russell M. Nelson, "Partners in the Work," address to Relief Society General Board, February 26, 1987.
65. Dale G. Renlund, "That I Might Draw All Men unto Me," *Ensign*, May 2016.
66. "I Stand All Amazed," *Hymns*, no. 193.
67. Renlund, "That I Might Draw All Men."

CHAPTER 5: "ENDOWED WITH PRIESTHOOD POWER": CONNECTING WOMEN WITH PRIESTHOOD IN THE TEMPLE AND HOME

1. J Ballard Washburn, "The Temple Is a Family Affair," *Ensign*, May 1995.
2. Linda K. Burton, "Priesthood: 'A Sacred Trust to Be Used for the Benefit

# NOTES

of Men, Women, and Children,'" Brigham Young University Women's Conference address, May 3, 2013.

3. Russell M. Nelson, "The Price of Priesthood Power," *Ensign*, May 2016; Doctrine and Covenants 84:19–20.
4. M. Russell Ballard, "Women of Dedication, Faith, Determination, and Action," Brigham Young University Women's Conference address, May 1, 2015.
5. Sheri Dew, *Women and the Priesthood: What One Mormon Woman Believes* (Salt Lake City: Deseret Book, 2013), 125.
6. Dew, *Women and the Priesthood*, 125.
7. Joseph Fielding Smith, *Doctrines of Salvation*, 3 vols., comp. Bruce R. McConkie (Salt Lake City: Bookcraft, 1956), 3:143.
8. Neil L. Andersen, "Power in the Priesthood," *Ensign*, November 2013.
9. David B. Haight, "Temples and Work Therein," *Ensign*, November 1990.
10. Ezra Taft Benson, *The Teachings of Ezra Taft Benson* (Salt Lake City: Deseret Book, 1988), 256.
11. David B. Haight, "Come to the House of the Lord," *Ensign*, May 1992.
12. Glenn L. Pace, "Spiritual Revival," *Ensign*, November 1992.
13. Joseph Fielding Smith, *Doctrines of Salvation*, 2:242.
14. Theodore M. Burton, "Salvation for the Dead—A Missionary Activity," *Ensign*, May 1975.
15. Dallin H. Oaks, "Priesthood Authority in the Family and the Church," *Ensign*, November 2005.
16. It may be important for some to note that during the early days of Church history, women performed blessings of healing that are done today only by men who are ordained to the office of elder. For a more comprehensive understanding of this topic, see Jill Mulvay Derr, Janath Russell Cannon, and Maureen Ursenback Beecher, *Women of Covenant: The Story of Relief Society* (Salt Lake City: Deseret Book, 1992).
17. Henry B. Eyring, "Families under Covenant," *Ensign*, May 2012.
18. Russell M. Nelson, "Celestial Marriage," *Ensign*, November 2008; Moroni 10:32; Doctrine and Covenants 93:19; see also Doctrine and Covenants 66:2; 93:13–14; 132:5–6.
19. Charles W. Penrose, in Conference Report, April 1921, 198.
20. Russell M. Nelson, "Protect the Spiritual Power Line," *Ensign*, November 1984; Doctrine and Covenants 132:19; emphasis added.
21. L. Tom Perry, "Fatherhood, an Eternal Calling," *Ensign*, May 2004; Gordon B. Hinckley, "This Thing Was Not Done in a Corner," *Ensign*, November 1996.
22. "The Family: A Proclamation to the World," *Ensign*, November 2010.
23. Russell M. Nelson, "Be Prepared to Explain Our Religion," Priesthood Leadership Conference, Barrigada, Guam, February 23, 2013.
24. Gordon B. Hinckley, "Our Solemn Responsibilities," *Ensign*, November 1991.
25. Gordon B. Hinckley, "Women of the Church," *Ensign*, November 1996.

## NOTES

26. Spencer W. Kimball, *The Teachings of Spencer W. Kimball*, ed. Edward L. Kimball (Salt Lake City: Bookcraft, 1982), 316.
27. Russell M. Nelson, "Endure and Be Lifted Up," *Ensign*, May 1997; see Doctrine and Covenants 42:22.
28. James E. Faust, "The Prophetic Voice," *Ensign*, May 1996.
29. M. Russell Ballard, "The Sacred Responsibilities of Parenthood," *Ensign*, March 2006.
30. Ballard, "Sacred Responsibilities."
31. Ballard, "Sacred Responsibilities."
32. Dale G. Renlund and Ruth Lybbert Renlund, *The Melchizedek Priesthood: Understanding the Doctrine, Living the Principles* (Salt Lake City: Deseret Book, 2018), 23.
33. Russell M. Nelson, "Our Sacred Duty to Honor Women," *Ensign*, May 1999; Ephesians 5:25.
34. Russell M. Nelson, *Teachings of Russell M. Nelson* (Salt Lake City: Deseret Book, 2018), 200.
35. Tad Walch, "Elder Holland Answers Questions from Young, Married Latter-day Saints in Anglican Oxford Chapel," *Church News*, November 28, 2018; https://www.churchofjesuschrist.org/church/news/elder-holland-answers-questions-from-young-married-latter-day-saints-in-anglican-oxford-chapel?lang=eng.
36. Russell M. Nelson, "Nurturing Marriage," *Ensign*, May 2006.
37. Russell M. Nelson, "Lessons from Eve," *Ensign*, November 1987.
38. Taken from comments on motherhood from Sister Julie B. Beck, general conference training, October 2009.
39. Julie B. Beck, Brigham Young University Women's Conference address, May 2011.
40. John A. Widtsoe, *Evidences and Reconciliations* (Salt Lake City: Bookcraft, 1960), 244.
41. Russell M. Nelson, "Sisters' Participation in the Gathering of Israel," *Ensign*, November 2018.
42. Hugh B. Brown, *Continuing the Quest* (Salt Lake City: Deseret Book, 1961), 7.
43. "Message of the First Presidency," in Conference Report, October 1942, 12–13; read by President J. Reuben Clark Jr.
44. Russell M. Nelson, "Ministering with the Power and Authority of God," *Ensign*, May 2018.
45. Henry B. Eyring, "Women and Gospel Learning in the Home," *Ensign*, November 2018; "The Family: A Proclamation to the World," 129.
46. Henry B. Eyring, *To Draw Closer to God: A Collection of Discourses* (Salt Lake City: Deseret Book, 1997), 143.
47. Joseph F. Smith, *Gospel Doctrine*, 5th ed. (Salt Lake City: Deseret Book, 1939), 300.

# NOTES

## CHAPTER 6: THAT WE MIGHT BE ONE

1. Henry B. Eyring, "That We May Be One," *Ensign,* May 1998.
2. Gérald Caussé, "Ye Are No More Strangers," *Ensign,* November 2013.
3. Mother Teresa, in R. M. Lala, *A Touch of Greatness: Encounters with the Eminent* (New York: Viking, 2001), x.
4. Thomas S. Monson, "Charity Never Faileth," *Ensign,* November 2010; Mother Teresa, in Lala, *Touch of Greatness,* x; John 15:12.
5. The Joseph Smith Papers, "Nauvoo Relief Society Minute Book," p. [10], https://josephsmithpapers.org/paper-summary/nauvoo-relief-society-minute-book/7.
6. "Nauvoo Relief Society Minute Book," p. [52].
7. "Nauvoo Relief Society Minute Book," p. [62].
8. "Nauvoo Relief Society Minute Book," p. [62].
9. Julie B. Beck, "And upon the Handmaids in Those Days Will I Pour Out My Spirit," *Ensign,* May 2010.
10. M. Russell Ballard, "Women of Dedication, Faith, Determination, and Action," Brigham Young University Women's Conference address, May 1, 2015.
11. James E. Faust, "Heirs to the Kingdom of God," *Ensign,* May 1995.
12. Bonnie L. Oscarson, "Sisterhood: Oh, How We Need Each Other," *Ensign,* May 2014.
13. "As Sisters in Zion," *Hymns,* no. 309.
14. Thomas S. Monson, "Charity Never Faileth," *Ensign,* November 2010.
15. This statement was given by Lucy Mack Smith, in "Nauvoo Relief Society Minute Book," [19].
16. *Handbook 2: Administering the Church* (Salt Lake City: The Church of Jesus Christ of Latter-day Saints, 2010), 5.1.
17. Bonnie L. Oscarson, "Young Women in the Work," *Ensign,* May 2018.
18. Oscarson, "Young Women in the Work"; *Handbook 2,* 10.3.1.
19. John A. Widtsoe, *Priesthood and Church Government* (Salt Lake City: Deseret Book, 1939), 93.
20. Jean B. Bingham, "Ministering as the Savior Does," *Ensign,* May 2018.
21. M. Russell Ballard, "Let Us Think Straight," Brigham Young University Devotional, August 20, 2013; speeches.byu.edu.
22. M. Russell Ballard, "Strength in Counsel," *Ensign,* November 1993.
23. First Presidency letter, August 19, 2015.
24. Joan Chittister, "We are at a crossroads for women in the church," *National Catholic Reporter,* December 11, 2013; https://www.ncronline.org/blogs/where-i-stand/we-are-crossroads-women-church.
25. Russell M. Nelson, "Sisters' Participation in the Gathering of Israel," *Ensign,* November 2018; Russell M. Nelson, "A Plea to My Sisters," *Ensign,* November 2015; emphasis added.
26. "The Relief Society Declaration," *The Latter-day Saint Woman: Basic Manual for Women, Part A* (Salt Lake City: The Church of Jesus Christ of Latter-day Saints, 2000), xi.

## NOTES

27. *Handbook 2*, 19.1.2.
28. Jill Mulvay Derr, Janath Russell Cannon, and Maureen Ursenback Beecher, *Women of Covenant: The Story of Relief Society* (Salt Lake City: Deseret Book, 1992), 42.
29. Russell M. Nelson, "Partners in the Work," address to Relief Society General Board, February 26, 1987.
30. Russell M. Nelson, "'Set in Order Thy House,'" *Ensign*, November 2001; Doctrine and Covenants 132:19.
31. Derr, Cannon, and Beecher, *Women of Covenant*, 37.

CHAPTER 7: FILLING THE MEASURE OF OUR CREATION

1. Russell M. Nelson, "A Plea to My Sisters," *Ensign*, November 2015.
2. Russell M. Nelson, "Sisters' Participation in the Gathering of Israel," *Ensign*, November 2018.
3. Dieter F. Uchtdorf, "Your Potential, Your Privilege," *Ensign*, May 2011.
4. Russell M. Nelson, "Becoming True Millennials," Worldwide Devotional for Young Adults, January 10, 2016; broadcasts.churchofjesuschrist.org.
5. M. Russell Ballard, "Let Us Think Straight," Brigham Young University Devotional, August 20, 2013; speeches.byu.edu.
6. M. Russell Ballard, "Women of Dedication, Faith, Determination, and Action," Brigham Young University Women's Conference address, May 1, 2015.
7. *Teachings of Presidents of the Church: Joseph F. Smith* (Salt Lake City: The Church of Jesus Christ of Latter-day Saints, 1998), 184.
8. Belle S. Spafford, "Reaching Every Facet of a Woman's Life: A Conversation with Belle S. Spafford, Relief Society General President," *Ensign*, June 1974.
9. Gordon B. Hinckley, "How Can I Become the Woman of Whom I Dream?" *Ensign*, May 2001.
10. Gordon B. Hinckley, Remarks, National Press Club, March 8, 2000; quoted in *Discourses of Gordon B. Hinckley*, 2 vols. (Salt Lake City: Deseret Book, 2004–2005), 2:460.
11. Eliza R. Snow, in *Evening News*, January 14, 1870.
12. Sheri Dew, *Women and the Priesthood: What One Mormon Woman Believes* (Salt Lake City: Deseret Book, 2013), 125.
13. Spencer W. Kimball, "The Role of Righteous Women," *Ensign*, November 1979.
14. Linda S. Reeves, "Protection from Pornography—a Christ-Focused Home," *Ensign*, May 2014.
15. Russell M. Nelson, "Woman—Of Infinite Worth," *Ensign*, November 1989.
16. Nelson, "A Plea to My Sisters."
17. Nelson, "A Plea to My Sisters."

# INDEX

Aaronic Priesthood: during time of Moses, 17; restoration of, 19–20; offices of, 28; and keys of ministering of angels, 33–35
Abraham, 15–16
Adam and Eve, 13–15, 99, 107
Andersen, Neil L., 50, 94
Andersen, Wilford W., 86
Angels, keys of ministering of, 33–35
Anger, 100
Anointings, 70–71
Apostasy, 18–19
Apostolic keys, 31, 35, 78
"As Sisters in Zion," 117
Atonement, 14, 27, 41
Authority. *See* Priesthood authority

Ballard, M. Russell: on access to power and blessings of priesthood, xi; on healing through priesthood, 4; on Heavenly Mother, 10; on eternal nature of family, 22–23; on priesthood keys, 29; on ministering of angels, 34; on blessings of priesthood, 52, 80; on unrevealed knowledge regarding women and priesthood, 63–64; on temple ordinances, 70; on power of God, 80; on blessings of temple, 82; on priesthood authority of women, 92; on family roles, 102–3; on receiving revelation, 115; on involving sisters in councils, 122; on need for faithful women, 132; on diversity of women, 133

Beck, Julie B., 9, 41, 108, 115
Benson, Ezra Taft, 4, 15, 17, 20, 66
Bingham, Jean B., 121–22
Bishop(s): and priesthood keys of presidency, 33, 57–58; and young women, 121
Boundaries, priesthood keys of presidency limited by, 56–57. *See also* Jurisdiction; Stewardship(s)
Brown, Hugh B., 108
Burton, Linda K., 81, 89

Callings: priesthood authority through, 29, 47–49; equality of priesthood authority through, 49–50; priesthood keys of presidency and timing of, 58–59; women's influence on men in, 61; and sustaining those with priesthood keys, 123–24; in premortal existence, 136
Callister, Tad R., 80–81
Cannon, George Q., 81
Caussé, Gérald, 113
Charity, 116–18, 127–28
Chittister, Joan, 122
Christofferson, D. Todd, 80

# INDEX

Church of Jesus Christ of Latter-day Saints, The: as priesthood administrative structure, 6–7, 22–23; function of priesthood in family versus, 26–27, 95; priesthood authority in, 27–29; order and organizational structure of, 37–40; priesthood power in, 41–44; Relief Society and organization of, 62–63; need for both men and women in, 63; temple and organization of, 67; and interfaith unity, 113
Community of Christ, 84–85, 113
Confidentiality, 60
Councils, 122
Covenants: and keys of ministering of angels, 33–35; priesthood power through, 61–62; and unity with Christ, 125–26
Creation, 107
Cruise, parable of, 130–31

Deacons, duties of, 28
Dead, ordinances for, 75–76, 82–84
Degrees of glory, 73–74
Derr, Jill, 124
Dew, Sheri, xiii, 71–72, 92–93, 136
Diversity, 133–34
Divine nature, 11–13, 93–94
Doctrine, understanding true, xiv
Dogs, rescue of abandoned, 126–27

Elders, duties of, 28
Elders quorum, combining efforts of Relief Society and, 121–22
Elephant analogy, 7–9
Elias, 20
Elijah, 17–18, 20, 78
Endowment, 71–73, 77, 92, 93
Entitlement, 86
Eve, 13–14, 99, 107
Exaltation, 69, 73, 74, 76, 93
Exceptions, 117
Eyring, Henry B., 14, 76, 95, 109, 112

Fall of Adam, 14
Family: as priesthood administrative structure, 6–7; eternal nature of, 22–24; function of priesthood in Church versus, 26–27, 95; link between priesthood and, 88; priesthood power lost through unrighteousness in, 100–110; women's role in, 102–3, 107–10; men's role in, 102–6; as priority, 110–11; unity within, 125. *See also* Home; Marriage; Patriarchal/familial priesthood structure; Sealing
"Family: A Proclamation to the World, The," 11–12, 98, 102
Fathers, role of, 102–6. *See also* Men
Fault finding, 114–15
Faust, James E., 102, 116

Garment, 70
Geography, priesthood keys of presidency limited by, 56–57
Glory, degrees of, 73–74
God: power of, 9, 72, 79, 80, 81, 93–94, 107; and Heavenly Mother, 9–10; and patriarchal order, 11; becoming like, 12–13; keys of knowledge of, 78–79; women and presence of, 80; knowing will of, 132

Hales, Robert D., 70
Hallstrom, Donald L., 37
Healing, through priesthood, 3–4
Heavenly Mother, 9–13
Hierarchical/ecclesiastical priesthood structure, 6–7; from Christ's mortal ministry to Apostasy, 18–19; from Restoration to today, 19–23; author's testimony of, 25–26
Hinckley, Gordon B., 81, 98, 99, 100, 135
Holland, Jeffrey R., xiii, 105–6
Holy Ghost, knowing will of God through, 132
Home: significance of, 88; changing nature of, 88–89; structured in order of patriarchal government, 89–90;

# INDEX

temple and priesthood power in, 92–95. *See also* Family; Marriage; Patriarchal/familial priesthood structure; Sealing
Hubble, Mrs., 38–39

Initiatory ordinance, 70–71
Israel, gathering of, 16, 63, 75–76, 122–23

Jack, Elaine, 122
Jesus Christ: Atonement of, 14, 27, 41; and hierarchical/ecclesiastical priesthood structure, 18; mortal mission of, 41; taking upon name of, 76–77; unity with, 125–27
Judging others, 114
Jurisdiction: priesthood authority limited by, 51–52; priesthood keys of presidency and, 53–56. *See also* Stewardship(s)

Keys. *See* Priesthood keys
Kimball, Heber C., xv
Kimball, Spencer W., 1–5, 66, 101, 136
Kirtland Temple, 20
Knowledge of God, keys of, 78–79
Kofford, Cree-L, 74

Learning: continual, 65–66; in temple, 90
Lee, Harold B., 10
Los Angeles California Temple visitors' center, author receives mission call to, 53–56

Marriage: new and everlasting covenant of, xi, 4, 66, 69, 73–75; and applicability of priesthood keys of presidency, 59–60; and women's priesthood authority, 72–73; sealing and, 73–74; equal partnership in, 98–100; covenant relationship in, 101–3. *See also* Family; Home; Patriarchal/familial priesthood structure; Sealing
Maxwell, Neal A., xiii, 41

McConkie, Bruce R., xiv, 16, 18, 69, 77
McConkie, Carol F., 82
McKay, David O., 65
Melchizedek Priesthood: removed from earth, 17, 18–19; restoration of, 19–20; offices of, 28; temple ordinances associated with, 67–68; knowledge of mysteries of kingdom through, 79
Member missionary work, 119–20
Men: as "priesthood," 50–51; women's influence on, in callings, 61; needed in Church, 63; equality of women and, 77; roles of, in family, 102–6; unity between women and, 121–23. *See also* Fathers, role of
Millet, Robert, 11, 16
Ministering, 57
Missionaries and missionary work, priesthood authority and, 47–49, 53–56
Monson, Thomas S., 81, 114, 117–18
Moses, 17, 20
Mother(s): Spencer W. Kimball comforts, 1–5; presiding in home, 26–27, 107; illness and death of author's, 101–2; role of, 102–3, 107–10; influence of, 126–27; follows prompting to save author, 129–30. *See also* Women
Mother's Day, 115
Mother Teresa, 114
Mysteries of the kingdom, keys of, 78–79

Nauvoo Temple, 66–67, 91
Nelson, Dantzel White, 133
Nelson, Russell M.: on gospel knowledge, xiii; on stepping forward, xiv–xvi; on stretching to receive personal revelation, xv–xvi; on understanding priesthood power and authority, 5, 79; on priesthood and sealing, 11; on patriarchal order of priesthood, 15; on Apostasy, 18–19; on importance of women, 24; on priesthood power, 41, 42; on women supporting men in callings, 61; on priesthood power and

# INDEX

authority of women, 62; on temple ordinances, 69, 85–86; on women and endowment, 72; on women and gathering of Israel, 76, 122–23; on blessings of temple, 81, 83; on ordinances for dead, 82; on learning in temple, 90; on blessings of temple marriage, 96, 97; on division of labor in marriage, 98–99; on marriage, 101, 125; on men's role in family, 104–5, 106; on creative power of priesthood, 107; on mothers, 108; on women and nurturing, 109; on unity among men and women in Church, 124; on importance of eternal family, 125; on influence of women, 130; on need for faithful women, 130; on spiritual gifts of women, 130; on women of this dispensation, 130; on knowing will of God, 132; on divine mission of women, 136–37

Nelson, Wendy Watson, 133

New and everlasting covenant of marriage, xi, 4, 66, 69, 73–75. *See also* Patriarchal/familial priesthood structure

Nurturing, 107–10

"O My Father," 10

Oaks, Dallin H.: on priesthood in family versus Church, 6–7, 59, 60, 95; on heavenly parents, 10; on family in plan of salvation, 11; on function of priesthood in family versus Church, 26; on women presiding in home, 26, 107; on women and priesthood authority, 29; on Aaronic Priesthood and keys of ministering of angels, 34; on order in Church organization, 39; on men and priesthood, 50; on priesthood authority and keys, 53; on geographic boundaries and priesthood authority, 56; on priesthood authority to call and release, 58–59; on organization of Relief Society, 62; on putting reasons to revelation, 63; on taking upon name of Christ, 76–77

Oaks, June Dixon, 133

Oaks, Kristen McMain, 133

Oath and covenant of the priesthood, 89–92

Offense, xiii

Order, in Church, 37–39

Ordinances. *See* Endowment; Initiatory ordinance; Sacrament; Temple ordinances

Ordination, priesthood authority through, 28

Oscarson, Bonnie L., 63, 116, 120, 121

Pace, Glenn L., 11

Packer, Boyd K., xiv, 23, 63, 65–66, 78

Page, Hiram, 38

Paper route, 129–30

Partnership: and applicability of priesthood keys of presidency, 59–60; marriage as equal, 98–100

Patriarchal/familial priesthood structure, 6–7, 11; Ezra Taft Benson on, 4; from Adam and Eve to Abraham, 13–16; from Moses to Elijah, 17–18; and focus on family, 22–24; and history of temple and priesthood in this dispensation, 66–68; and purpose of temple, 69; and sealing ordinance, 74–75, 97; and priesthood keys in temple, 77–80; home structured in order of, 89–90; priesthood keys in, 95. *See also* Family; Home; Marriage; New and everlasting covenant of marriage; Sealing

Pearce, Virginia, 71

Penrose, Charles W., 97

Perfection, 96–97

Perry, L. Tom, 98

Perspective, 123–24

Peruvian carpet cleaner, 126–27

Pioneer trek, 49–50, 118–19

Plan of salvation: priesthood in context of, 9–13, 27–28; Fall as part of, 14

# INDEX

Pregnant woman, Spencer W. Kimball comforts, 1–5

Premortal existence, 136

Presidency, priesthood keys of, 31–33, 36, 53–61, 95

Presiding: of women in home, 26–27, 107; and equality in priesthood authority, 49–50; gender and, 50; of men in home, 100–101, 103–6

Priesthood: questions regarding, x–xi, 45–46; blessings of, for women, xi; teaching truths regarding, xi–xii; understanding, xii–xiii, 5–9; living up to privileges of, xv, 5, 130–32; used to bless righteous disciples, 1–5; healing through, 3–4; order of, 4; definitions and use of term, 5–6; administrative structures of, 6–7; in context of plan of salvation, 9–13, 27–28; and sealing of families, 11; restoration of, 19–20; fulness of, 20, 69; men as, 50–51; recipients of blessings of, 52–53, 80; unrevealed knowledge regarding women and, 63–64; and temple in this dispensation, 66–68; link between family and, 88; oath and covenant of, 89–92. *See also* Aaronic Priesthood; Hierarchical/ecclesiastical priesthood structure; Melchizedek Priesthood; Patriarchal/familial priesthood structure; Priesthood authority; Priesthood keys; Priesthood power

Priesthood authority, 25–27; understanding, 5, 79; in hierarchical/ecclesiastical priesthood structure, 21; to perform ordinances, 21; in Church, 27–29; transparency in delegation of, 37–40, 43; recipients of blessings of, 47, 52–53; received by women, 47–49, 72–73, 92; limited by jurisdiction, 51–52; limited by time, 52; in temple, 76–77; received from temple, 92; in family, 95; received in sealing ordinance, 95–97

Priesthood keys, 29–37; restoration of, 19–20; and exercise of priesthood authority, 29; defined, 30–31; apostolic, 31, 35, 78; of presidency, 31–33, 36, 53–61, 95; general, 33–35, 36; purpose of, 37; transparency in delegation of, 37–40, 43; limited by stewardship, 53–56; boundaries limiting, 56–57; limited by time, 57–58; and timing of calls and releases, 58–59; in temple, 77–80; held by temple president, 78; of mysteries of kingdom / knowledge of God, 78–79; in patriarchal structure, 95; sustaining those with, 123–24

Priesthood power: understanding, 5, 79; in Church, 41–44; through covenants, 61–62; from righteousness, 81; received in temple, 92–95; received in sealing ordinance, 95–97; lost through unrighteousness in family, 100–110

Rebekah, 16

Reeves, Linda S., 136

Releases, priesthood keys of presidency and timing of, 58–59

Relief Society: organization of, 62–63, 68; combining efforts of elders quorum and, 121–22; purpose of, 127–28

Renlund, Dale G., 5, 19, 41, 61, 75, 82–83, 86, 103–4, 133–34

Renlund, Ruth Lybbert, 5, 19, 61, 75, 103–4, 133–34

Restoration of gospel, and organization of Relief Society, 62

Revelation: stretching ability to receive, xv–xvi; order in reception of, 38–40; determining origins of, 39; and knowledge regarding women and priesthood, 63–64; importance of ability to qualify for and act on, 115. *See also* Stewardship(s)

Righteousness: as prerequisite to priesthood power, 42–44; power from, 81; priesthood power lost

through unrighteousness in family, 100–110
Rock Creek Hollow, 105
Romney, Marion G., 39
Roommate, difficult, becomes author's mission companion, 53–56

Sacrament, 76–77
Sarah, 15–16
Sealing, 11, 73–75, 78, 95–97. *See also* Family; Home; Marriage; Patriarchal/familial priesthood structure
Setting apart, priesthood authority through, 29, 47–50
Sister missionaries, priesthood authority of, 47–49
Smith, Bathsheba W., 68
Smith, Joseph: on living up to privileges, xv; on nature of God, 12; on Fall, 14; on priesthood keys, 19; and restoration of priesthood, 19–20; on Elijah, 20; and priesthood structures, 20–21; and organizational structure of Church, 38–39; and organization of Relief Society, 62, 68; on temple, 66–67; and restoration of temple ordinances, 67–68; on God's accessibility to women, 80; on judging others, 114–15; on purpose of Relief Society, 127–28; on women taking their places, 137
Smith, Joseph F., 110, 135
Smith, Joseph Fielding, 73, 93
Snow, Eliza R., 10, 136
Snow, Erastus, 9–10
Spafford, Belle S., 135
Spiritual gifts, 130
Spouse, priesthood keys of presidency as not applicable to, 59–60
Stewardship(s): priesthood authority limited by, 51–52; priesthood keys of presidency and, 53–56; in family, 102
Success, 115

Talmage, James E., 12–13, 71, 72–73

Temple: and patriarchal order of priesthood, 15; role of women in, 66; and priesthood in this dispensation, 66–68; purpose of, 69; priesthood authority in, 76–77; priesthood keys in, 77–80; blessings of, 81–84, 85–87; learning in, 90; priesthood authority received from, 92; priesthood power received from, 92–95
Temple garment, 70
Temple ordinances, 69–76; sealing, 11, 73–75, 78, 95–97; of heavenly parents, 12; and continual learning, 65–66; restoration of, 67–68; and exaltation, 69; initiatory, 70–71; endowment, 71–73, 77, 92, 93; for dead, 75–76, 82–84; priesthood power received from, 80–81, 92–95
Temple president, keys held by, 78
Time: priesthood authority limited by, 52; priesthood keys of presidency limited by, 57–58
Twins, rescued from garbage dump, 127
Uchtdorf, Dieter F., 130–31
Unity, 112–13, 127–28; between men and women at church, 63, 121–23; in marriage, 98–100; calls for, in scriptures, 112; in Zion, 112–13; among all people of faith, 113; between women, 113–14; with young women, 118–21; and sustaining those with priesthood keys, 123–24; within family, 125; with Christ, 125–27
Unrighteousness, priesthood power lost through, 100–110
UPS delivery, 86

Washburn, J Ballard, 88
Washings and anointings, 70–71
Widtsoe, John A., 10, 75, 80, 84, 108, 121
Women: blessings of priesthood for, xi; importance of, 24; presiding in home, 26–27, 107; priesthood authority given to, 29, 47–49, 72–73, 92; questions regarding priesthood

# INDEX

and, 45–46; influence of, on men in callings, 61; priesthood power given to, 61–62, 92–95; needed in Church, 63; unrevealed knowledge regarding priesthood and, 63–64; role of, in temple, 66; and gathering of Israel, 76, 122–23; equality of men and, 77; ordained, in Community of Christ, 84–85; roles of, in family, 102–3, 107–10; unity between, 113–14; unity between young women and, 118–21; unity between men and, 121–23; in councils, 122; need for faithful, 130, 132–33; spiritual gifts of, 130; diversity among, 133–34; limiting service opportunities of, 134–35; opportunities open to, 135; as leaders, 135–36; premortal assignments of, 136; divine mission of, 136–37. *See also* Mother(s)

Woodruff, Wilford, 12

Young, Brigham, 12, 71, 78

Young women: unity with, 118–20; experiences for preparation of, 120–21; spiritual needs of, 132–33

Zion, 112–13